The Insider's Guide to Foster Care

of related interest

My Life After Trauma Handbook
Surviving and Thriving Using Psychological Approaches
Bridie Gallagher, Sue Knowles, Reggie Worthington and Jade Baron
Illustrated by Chloe Collett
ISBN 978 1 83997 128 0
eISBN 978 1 83997 129 7

My Intense Emotions Handbook
Manage Your Emotions and Connect Better with Others
Sue Knowles, Bridie Gallagher and Hannah Bromley
Illustrated by Emmeline Pidgen
Foreword by Kim Golding
ISBN 978 1 78775 382 2
eISBN 978 1 78775 383 9

The A–Z of Therapeutic Parenting
Strategies and Solutions
Sarah Naish
ISBN 978 1 78592 376 0
eISBN 978 1 78450 732 9
Audio ISBN 978 1 52937 496 4

Raising Kids with Big, Baffling Behaviors
Brain-Body-Sensory Strategies that Really Work
Robyn Gobbel
ISBN 978 1 83997 428 1
eISBN 978 1 83997 429 8
Audio ISBN 978 1 39981 631 1

The INSIDER'S GUIDE to FOSTER CARE

What Care Leavers Need You to Know

Kim Emenike, Caydin Jay,
and **Amy Baker**

Edited by
Dr Sue Knowles and **Dr Laura Lever**

Foreword by Fatima Whitbread MBE

Illustrated by Richard Hayward

Jessica Kingsley Publishers
London and Philadelphia

First published in Great Britain in 2025 by Jessica Kingsley Publishers
An imprint of John Murray Press

2

A CIP catalogue record for this title is available from the
British Library and the Library of Congress

ISBN 978 1 80501 349 5
eISBN 978 1 80501 350 1

Printed and bound in the United States by Integrated Books International

Jessica Kingsley Publishers' policy is to use papers that are natural, renewable and recyclable products and made from wood grown in sustainable forests. The logging and manufacturing processes are expected to conform to the environmental regulations of the country of origin.

Jessica Kingsley Publishers
Carmelite House
50 Victoria Embankment
London EC4Y 0DZ

www.jkp.com

John Murray Press
Part of Hodder & Stoughton Ltd
An Hachette Company

The authorised representative in the EEA is Hachette Ireland, 8 Castlecourt Centre, Dublin 15, D15 XTP3, Ireland (email: info@hbgi.ie)

Contents

Foreword

All children deserve to grow up in a happy home. This wasn't always my experience.

During childhood, I spent 14 years in care. I felt abandoned, and I had to cope with the emotional trauma that caused. At first, I didn't understand what had happened to my parents, and would ask, 'Is my mummy coming to collect me?' My time in care was lacking love and affection, and I was neglected. I found ways to protect myself by putting walls up, and I didn't allow myself to be loved in any way. As Amy, Kim, and Caydin (CJ) explore in Chapter 5, children in care have to find ways to protect themselves from getting hurt in relationships.

Children need stability, so that they can start to put down roots. As Chapter 2 discusses, moving to a new home is frightening, as everything you know is suddenly taken away from you and you need to start all over again in a new place. You lose your connections, your friends, and people who are important to you. And you don't even know whether it's worth trying, as you don't know if the new home will work out. So getting this right, making sure that young people have safe, stable homes, is essential.

One of the reasons why I've written the foreword for this book is that I experienced how much having one, or two, caregivers who really love and care for you can change your life. A lady who worked in the home where I lived, 'Auntie Rae', was the bright, shining star in my life. She protected me, helped me to survive, and gave me the love that I needed.

As this book explores in Chapter 8, school can be a lifesaver for children in care. For me, it was the only thing that stopped me from drowning. I was in trouble at school a lot, but despite this, I excelled at sport. One day, I saw a javelin on the floor and had the urge to pick it up. My new coach, Margaret, then taught me everything about the sport. When Margaret later fostered me at age 14, I finally felt that I had a family, that I belonged, I was loved, and I had a future.

Now, as a retired athlete, I want to use my platform to advocate for, and create awareness of, children in care. I want to give them a voice so that they are properly heard and valued within society. Through my UK campaign and the summit in 2025, I want to promote positive change through collaboration, to be an advocate for children in the care system, and to harness the power of one voice to improve the life outcomes of young people. This book allows young people in foster care to share their views and perspectives, on what they think needs to change, and what they want you, as foster carers, to know. I believe in these children, and I believe that you, as foster carers, have the chance to make a real difference.

Fatima Whitbread MBE
https://fatimascampaign.com

Preface

A note from the editors, Laura and Sue

We believe this book is important and very much needed. We wanted to support the writing of it, so that it could be created and could influence our everyday work. It's crucial that the work that we both do (as psychologists or carers) is first and foremost led by the needs and wants of the young people that we're trying to support.

There are many books out there written by 'professionals', people with fancy titles and job roles like us. Most books about 'therapeutic foster caring' are written by foster carers themselves, or those who have a background in therapy or social care. These can be really helpful; they can validate carers' experiences, and give good advice.

However, there's a danger that these 'adult-led' books written by professionals fail to capture the child's voice and those unique perspectives and experiences that you could never fully understand without facing them first hand. Who can advise foster carers about what it's like to be a child in care, and how to help, better than a care-experienced young person? And yet, these voices – the most important voices – are missing.

We wanted to create space for these voices of people who are often unheard in the published world, people who know first hand what it's like to be in foster care, to describe what matters to them, and what adults might need to understand. We are so grateful to them for sharing their wisdom, and we hope it helps you in your journey as foster carers.

The contents of this book were proposed by its authors CJ, Amy, and Kim, as they reflected on what they felt was most important for foster carers to know. For each chapter, the content is written by the three authors, but also contains reflections, thoughts and perspectives, stories, and quotes from 13 additional care-experienced people who were consulted throughout the writing of this book (as named in the acknowledgements at the end of the book).

As editors, we have helped to pull all the voices together into a narrative with recommendations, which have then been reviewed and agreed by the author group.

The language and terminology used throughout this book is the preferred language of the authors, CJ, Kim, and Amy, and the other young people who have contributed to the book.

As clinical psychologists who work with young people in care or leaving care, and their parents, carers, teachers, social workers, and wider systems, we know that each relationship is important and has the power to support young people to survive and thrive. Each young person is different, with their own quirks, resourcefulness, and unique take on the world, as is every adult they meet.

We want to support you as adults to tune in to the needs, feelings, and strengths of these incredible young people, and find ways that fit with your own way of supporting them, guided by current thinking and evidence on working with young people in care or leaving care, and the unique insights captured by Kim, Amy, CJ, and the many other young people who have contributed to this book.

We know there's a lot of advice out there, particularly surrounding attachment and developmental trauma, and with the influx of social media narratives, it can feel overwhelming and intimidating to hear so many loud voices telling us how carers 'should' parent. There's no specific 'right' way to be a foster carer, and each person caring will bring their own strengths, resources, and personality.

However, understanding what it can be like to be a young person in foster care, and hearing their stories of what helps and hinders, can allow you to better tune in to your child's needs, to provide the best care you can. We hope this book will help you connect with your values in being a caring, compassionate, curious, and empathic person first and foremost.

CHAPTER 1

Introduction

We, Kim Emenike, Caydin Jay (CJ), and Amy Baker, are the authors of this book.

We wrote this book to support those caring for young people in foster care, and enable them to better understand what it's like to be in the care system and what you can do to help. There are so many other books out there, but they are usually written by professionals, or foster carers, rather than those who have lived experience of what it's actually like to be fostered.

The book also features a number of other young people and adults who have contributed their thoughts, views, reflections, and stories to this book – as you read through you will encounter Angel, Noor, Amy J, Diego, Dave, Mike S, Rosie, Shannon, Jo, Zoe, Zena, Zahra, Terry, and Mia, all of whom have valuable experiences and advice to share with you.

The insights shared within this book have come from authors with a diverse range of experiences of living in foster care. We understand what it's like to be in foster care, the challenges, and the real potential for how the relationships that are built between a child and their foster carers can make such a positive difference.

Through this book we hope that you will better understand what your child could experience through their time in the care system and be better prepared to know how to best support them.

The reality of foster care

When a child turns 14, they're usually worried about things like who they've fallen out with at school, whether their new hairstyle fits in, the pressure of exams, or embarrassing themselves in front of the person they have a crush on.

The reality is often so different for young people living in foster care. They might well have the usual teenage worries, but these exist alongside other worries and stresses, such as whether their parents, brothers, and sisters are okay and when they'll see them again, where they'll be living next, and whether it's their fault they are in care.

Their day-to-day lives could be full of uncertainty, loss, anger, and fear, and they might have some difficult and confusing memories about their past that play over and over in their heads on repeat. They may also have uncertainties as to whether their memories are fully true or not.

There's usually a lot of catching up on missed schoolwork too, whether it's because it's too hard to concentrate or because of all the changes in school they've been through, or the education they've missed.

It's likely that, at some point, your foster child has had a difficult and traumatic time. There will be a reason why they're no longer living with their parents. Yet even though these family relationships might have had their challenges, or even been abusive, being apart from their most familiar people and moving between homes, often more than once, is really hard. And as we know, our past life experiences have a big role in shaping who we become and how we view ourselves and other people we meet.

Why we have written this book

'I had lovely foster parents and was very lucky in that aspect. However, my experience of being a child in care is something that shaped the person I was then and even now as an adult, having been to university, gaining a degree in social work, and having my own family. I am very proud of my identity and although too old to be legally considered a care leaver, it's a title I still identify with today. I understand what it feels like to be a child in the system and would love to inspire other children and young people to reach for the stars, as

well as support the adults caring for them to do their very best.' (Amy)

'Being in the care system as a teenager gives you a lot of insight into what needs to change. So now I want to use all the experiences I had in my foster care placements to help guide anyone reading this book to share what can help.' (CJ)

'Growing up in foster care for ten years showed me how broken the system is and I am determined to be a driving force in fixing it. My mission is to ensure that anyone entering foster care in the future has a much better experience than I did. I envisage a system that creates equal opportunities and provides an environment where care-experienced individuals feel loved, supported, and empowered. They should never be subjected to negative connotations and stigmas associated with growing up in foster care. By sharing my story and providing advice in this book, I aim to demonstrate that young people who have grown up in care are unstoppable. They CAN and WILL achieve anything they set their minds to.' (Kim)

Considerations before becoming a foster carer

You might have picked up this book because you're already a foster carer and want to find out more about how you can support the children in your care (thank you for doing this). But we're also aware that you might have picked up this book because you're thinking about whether or not you are the right person to be a foster carer, or you might even be going through the foster care approval process right now and looking for some last-minute thoughts.

We think it's only fair to be honest and say that being a foster carer isn't always easy. We recognize how difficult being a foster carer can be. However, we can promise that you have a truly important role and will have a lasting impact on the children you care for. One of the worst things that can happen is when a foster carer takes on a child and then decides that they can no longer care for them. Or when a carer finds it too difficult and starts to resent the child. It is in these moments that we need you more, and we need you to remember that we didn't choose this.

We need you to be realistic. It might be great and fun and rewarding, but it's also going to be hard at times. Given the experiences that we're likely to have had before we came to you, you can't treat it as if it's a fresh start, because it's not. It might be to you, but for us, we don't have the option to leave our story behind.

Even if you're providing us with a good home, it's likely that you won't be able to solve everything for us. Unfortunately, even if you're providing the best care in the world, it doesn't necessarily mean that we will find it any easier.

You need to be willing to adapt to us and provide us with the care and support that we need.

So, it's important that you're sure that this is something you want to, and are able to do, before you welcome us into your life, because this matters and has the potential to change our lives too.

In this book, we share lots of experiences of what it's like to be a child in care, and what we need from those caring for us. We hope that once you've read this book, you are left thinking, *'I want to be a good foster carer; I want to do this.'*

How to use this book

We wrote this book as a pick-up-and-go practical resource for foster carers. That means that although you could read it front to back, each chapter can be a standalone resource to be dipped into when you need it, bringing together wide-ranging reflections, experiences, and anecdotes, alongside helpful prompts and ideas for you to try on each topic area.

In Chapter 2 (Going into a Stranger's Home), we consider what it's like for a young person meeting their foster carers and moving into a 'stranger's' home for the first time. The chapter includes lots of personal experiences and recommendations about what carers can do to help the young person to feel settled, respected, and comfortable.

Then in Chapter 3 (Understanding Us and Our Stories), we think about the importance of understanding, and holding, the story of the child. We talk about how you can start to have conversations with the child, at their pace, about their journeys and what's important to them. This understanding can help you to feel more connected to each other, and enable you to know more about who they are as an individual. We also carefully consider some of the challenges of having access to records and reports, and how this can be done well.

Chapter 4 (Building Relationships and Networks) describes the underlying loneliness that young people in care often experience, and thinks about what can cause and exacerbate this. Young people have so many transitions between homes, throughout education, between services, and this can lead to important relationships becoming fractured or ending. The young person can then feel left behind and really alone. Again, this topic is explored through quotes and themes, and then suggestions are made about how you can support young people to stay connected in their relationships, with their family, and wider networks, particularly given how important these relationships become as the child moves out of the care system as an adult.

Within Chapter 5 (Understanding What Healthy Relationships Look Like), we acknowledge that young people in care often have experienced difficult, unhealthy, or even abusive relationships growing up. Therefore, they might understandably find it hard to trust people, and they might not know what a healthy or good relationship really looks like. This chapter explores young people's understanding and experiences of the trickiness of relationships. It gives suggestions for how you can help young people learn what a 'good' relationship looks like, and how you can support them to build relationship skills.

Chapter 6 (Getting Through Difficult Days) focuses on how you can support your child through 'difficult days'. In this chapter, we recognize that there are several days throughout the year that might feel particularly difficult, such as birthdays, Mother's/Father's Day, Christmas, and anniversaries. We also think about how it's not just the day, but often the time around it, that can be a struggle. The chapter shares examples of and gives guidance on how you can best support your child through these difficult days, and how to show them love and grace at these times.

Chapter 7 (Supporting Us with Professional Networks) helps you to think about how to support your child when they're accessing other services. Within the chapter, we acknowledge that young people in care often have a range of services and professionals working with them, such as social care and mental health services. The chapter talks about young people's experiences of working with other services and how support from you as their carer can help, or hinder, their engagement. It explains that sometimes these appointments and meetings can feel like a 'tick-box' exercise; they can also be overly exposing and don't really listen to the needs of the child. Instead, the child ends up feeling treated differently from children still living with their parents, with a whole new level of expectations. We share ways that you can support your child to express their views and opinions, and we think about your role in the support offered by other services.

Chapter 8 (Education and Finding a Way Out of the System) builds on this by thinking specifically about how you can support your child in education. We highlight some of the key difficulties experienced by children in care in educational settings. We share examples and experiences, and think about what you, as a carer, can do to support your child. We also discuss the difficulties of making educational and vocational decisions, and how to support your child well through these.

In Chapter 9 (Leaving Home with Dignity), we acknowledge the difficult ways that young people often end up moving out of foster care, such as being 'given notice' that a placement is ending, or when they turn 18. We also talk about times when young people leave because they feel ready to, although the ending can still feel tough and bring up difficult feelings. We share young people's experiences of these endings, and then think about how you, as carers, can support young people to leave home in the most positive way possible, with dignity and respect.

In the last chapter of the book, Chapter 10 (Parting Words of Wisdom), we have some final messages from us (CJ, Kim, and Amy) and other young people, about what we would want you to hold in mind going forward.

Thank you for reading this book. The fact that you have chosen to read it is important in itself – it means that you want to hear our views and support the children in your care the best you can. And remember, you've got this.

The warmth of others' hope and love holding my heart.
They handle it gently, preparing for the worst
I've known some hands for years.
Some are new. But I trust these unlike other pairs.
For my wounds were never met with salt but
With lavender and honey instead.
I do not deserve this kindness yet they insist.
So I persist, to resist the circle being completed.
I wonder in this quest, am I defeated?
Or do I still have resolve to hold on for longer
This water is drowning me and I don't know if I have long left.
I'd still rather save them and sink like a stone
Than survive like I did – alone.

Excerpt from *Mea Ultimo*, a poem written by CJ

CHAPTER 2

Going into a Stranger's Home

Imagine that you've just been told that you're going to be moving house to live with a new foster family. You don't know where you're going, who you'll be living with, or what it'll be like. You have been given a bin bag, and told to put everything you own, all the things that matter to you, inside it. And that's if you're lucky and you haven't had to leave your personal belongings behind, or even had them refused to you by the people who are supposed to love you.

How would you be feeling? What would you choose to take? What would you choose to leave behind? What would you be thinking? What might you be worried about?

Try to imagine, just for a minute, what it might be like to try to start from scratch because of things you had zero control over.

This is the reality for many children going into care or moving from one foster home to another. The move can be sudden and unplanned, and feel absolutely terrifying as so much is unknown. The following chapter will help you to understand what it might be like for a child moving into your home for the first time, and to think about the preparations you can make to help them feel welcome, safer, and as if they belong.

> *My social worker said, 'Shall we get you a McDonald's before you go?' I always ate back then, but I didn't want it. I was so scared. I feel as traumatized about it now as I was back then. It's the scariest thing you go through as a kid. You don't know who you are living with; they could be murderers. It might sound silly, and I know Social Care do checks but, really, they could be anyone and you would never know. I had a lot of fears and they were never really addressed. I just had to live there until I made my own assessment that they were safe and not weird. I feel so awful for kids having to go through that.* (ANGEL)

'We have found you a placement'

For children old enough to be told they are moving in with a new foster family, the first words we hear are often something similar to, 'we have found you a placement'. As a child in care, like anyone else, we want a place that feels like home; a place where we can feel safe and just be ourselves; where we can relax and start to let our guard down; where we're accepted for who we are and don't feel judged.

Often it can take quite a lot for us to start to feel safe with you in your home. We might have had to move around a lot or have had bad experiences of living in foster care or with other adults. We might even have trusted and felt safe in a previous home, but something happened which meant we had to leave. This can make it hard for us to trust people, including you and your family. It might feel much safer not to trust and to keep people at a distance instead (we talk more about this in Chapter 5), keeping our guard up and our emotions in.

We might have found ways to keep ourselves safe by reading the room and trying to work out what and where the risks might be. It's likely that we might have low, or harsh, expectations of you and your home because of what we've experienced before. If we've moved a lot, we might also be wondering how long we'll realistically be with you before we have to move again.

For some of us, we could also really struggle with the idea of being part of a foster family, because we already have our own family, and we don't need another. If we already have a mum, a dad, siblings, and other blood relatives, then why do we need anyone else? Someone who's pretending to be our parent when we have the real thing?

We might wonder why we couldn't stay with our own family, if that's where we want to be. Or we might have had to grow up and look after ourselves so far, and therefore feel that we don't need anyone else.

Why are you telling me what to do? Why are you asking me this? Why are you coming up with a routine for me?

> *I was feeling angry all the time…because you can't see your mum, and don't understand why you can't see her or why you are having to live there and not be with your own family. You might be loyal to your mum and be thinking, why am I in care?* (DIEGO)

For these reasons, we might think that residential care is a better option for us, as it is 'a place to live' when we can't live with our family, rather than an attempt to 'replace' our family. Some of us believe this even more as we get older – we might understandably resist being part of a new family, and instead just want somewhere to live.

If we're moving to live with you but wanted to be in residential care, it can be helpful to know the reason for this decision, and for you to understand why this might be difficult for us. Even just saying you understand or 'get it' can help. It takes the pressure off.

> *I felt forced to be with them and in the foster system. In my country [of origin, Eritrea], we don't have a foster system. And then I learned that when I come here, I have to be with them, and like WHY? I thought I would be with friends I met in Calais, different refugees like me. I didn't want to be with a family. I had been homeless for over a year, seeing people dying and horrible things, and now suddenly I can't do so much. I had to follow rules. At the time, I just wanted*

> *to be an adult, because you don't have rules as an adult. I get it now that I understand safeguarding, but at that time I was like, but I survived worse like this, I will be fine.* (NOOR)

Some of us have always wanted a family and might not have experienced what it's like to be part of a family growing up. So, we might seek out love, care, and protection from you, and hold a sense of you as 'our new foster family'.

At the same time, it might feel scary. We might believe that there's no place for us in your home and we might feel like a burden invading your space. Maybe you won't like us, maybe you'll decide that you no longer want us to live with you, and we'll end up moving on again. This is especially hard if we have a sense that 'everyone always leaves' or 'everything is temporary'.

Moving into a ready-made family

> *It can be quite isolating moving in with a new family and you may not feel part of that family for a long time.* (AMY J)

It's really hard moving into a family that already exists. If you and your family have lived in your home a while, we can feel as if we're just a guest, intruding on someone else's home and life temporarily, because it's not really our home. It can feel even worse when there are photos on the walls and memories of your family's happy times together, but no photos or memories of us.

My foster parents and their family were amazing people, but by the time I reached them, I just needed somewhere to live. I had pretty much raised myself at that point and didn't feel that I fitted into any family, no matter how much love they gave me. (MIA)

It can complicate our feelings more when you have your own children (birth children, adopted children, or long-term foster children), especially at first. We might feel quite separate from the others, or fear that we're being treated differently, as you might prefer or feel closer to your other children.

I remember coming in and knowing nothing at all about their family. I thought I'm never gonna like it here. I'm really scared and anxious. I've no idea where I'm going or what's happening.

Even at age 12, I had no idea what was happening. I only met them once before moving in with them. I wish I'd have met them a few more times and I wish I'd have had more of a say about where I was going. My sister had a lot of say in who would be her next foster carer. I wasn't asked, 'What kind of couple do you want to live with?' or 'What do you want to see in a parent?' There was nothing about their hobbies, what kind of people they were. I didn't even know they had kids.

So it took me ages to speak to Gia. I was scared; there is an 18-year-old [Gia] here and they have blue hair. Then obviously we [Gia and I] became really close and ended up moving in together. But it would have helped if they'd have told me a bit about their family and their kids before we got there. (ANGEL)

No child is the same or has had the same journey, so if you compare us to other children or expect us to have had a similar journey, this can be counter-productive, and we might end up feeling like a failure.

For example, we won't all feel 'traumatized', and for some of us, showing pity can make us feel like a victim rather than helping us to feel strong. It's important to see us for who we are as individuals, and focus on our unique journey, story, and future. You can do this by asking us questions such as, 'What was that like?' rather than making assumptions about how we feel.

Sometimes even the label 'foster child' can get in the way. For some of us, it can feel soul crushing to be referred to as 'my foster child' when we've lived with a foster family most of our lives. This can lead us to feel that this home and family are still temporary. Perhaps our carers don't see us as part of their family really, and we therefore can't trust our carers to stick around with us into the future. Then again, others of us won't want to be called something different, so it's always better to ask.

It can be hard moving into a new family and you are not trying to be their family, but you're still there... I don't like them to assume I want to be part of their family, but I still want to do stuff with them, and to feel I belong, but I don't want a new family. So make me feel welcome, even though we both know we're not related, and let me know you are still going to be here for me and love me as a 'chosen' family. It's confusing for the young person, because they want to be part of the family, but want to be part of their own family too. (DIEGO)

I would have appreciated information about who they were, what they were like, and them asking me questions like, 'What do you want to see in a home?' Even if they weren't going to listen, it would have helped them to find out what kind of kid I was, what kind of household I would be comfortable in, my fears and anxieties. I had a lot going on in my head, but no one did anything to ease what was in my mind at the time by giving me reassurance, information, or asking questions. Maybe they thought I was too young. If they'd given more information about themselves, I would have been more comfortable. Maybe just a short story about them and their family – just write it down, to give it to the kids to share about them. Not dead formal, just something fun to make moving in feel like something exciting. (ANGEL)

A stranger's home

When we move into your home, everything can feel so unknown. It's as if we've moved to a new country and don't understand what the cultural unsaid rules are but know that everyone will look at us strangely if we don't follow them. It very much feels as if we've moved into a stranger's home; we've suddenly landed in someone else's house, so we are a guest, but also not a guest.

As a teenager, I initially didn't know if I had to ask them when I could leave my room, go into the garden, have breakfast, or even go to the toilet. I remember sitting on the couch, thinking that I needed the toilet, but then it felt really awkward not to ask, and to just get up and go. (AMY B)

It can feel awkward, scary, and even petrifying moving to live with a new family, whether we want to be there or not. There's so much that's uncertain, different, and new – unspoken rules, routines, and traditions that we know nothing about. It can be really hard to adjust and adapt quickly to our new reality.

It's difficult for us to know how we are expected to be and what's allowed. Essentially, each of us will have had a different background and experience of what home life looks like. For example, in your home, it might be fine for a child to help themselves to food from the fridge. But it might be that this wasn't allowed in our family home, or even our previous foster home, and we might have been told off for it. Even if you say, 'You don't have to ask', not asking might feel uncomfortable at first, and we might worry that we're doing something wrong. So these changes in rules can feel like a massive culture shock. It's hard to adjust.

Also, sometimes we might not know that our 'normal' isn't 'normal' to your everyday family. There might be things that we experienced in our childhood that we've always assumed happened in other families (such as physical punishment when we did something wrong, or not being allowed out of our rooms at night), so it feels very confusing to find out that this isn't a typical rule within a family home. It can then feel alien to try to fit into a new 'perfect' family situation.

Going into care actually made me notice and become aware of some of the abuse I had experienced when I lived at home with my dad and stepmum. Things like not being allowed to stroke the family dog unless there were people present, as well as being made to eat standing up unless it was an occasion, or being forced to eat all the sugary foods in the house because I took a can of pop that wasn't mine. Although this may sound obvious, this was normalized to me until I came into foster care, and so it felt bizarre to me that this wasn't how my foster carers did things. (MIA)

New home, new country, new language

Moving into a stranger's home can be hard enough, but it's so much harder when you're a refugee. You're in a completely new place, usually after quite a long journey to get there, not speaking the language or even knowing what to expect about your new home. Noor moved between four countries after leaving Eritrea and was 'internationally homeless' for one year. When she arrived in Kent, there was a new language to navigate, which she attempted using a combination of her own version of sign language, Google Translate, pictures, and an interpreter.

I arrived in 2015 as a refugee. I was a minor refugee, black and Muslim. There was a huge language barrier, which was challenging for me and my foster family, and we had to use sign language and Google Translate and find pictures. Because social services were worried I was here because of trafficking, they took my phone, so no social media, no connection. It was frustrating. Especially in the first couple of weeks, it's really hard for a kid when you know no one. We had technology but no human interaction with someone who spoke and understood the same language, to give reassurance. Speaking to an interpreter was a luxury, like when you are starving and you take the first bite of food. After weeks without speaking the same language, someone speaks and it's like, WOW. It can help minor refugees for you to find a community of people from a similar region, who might speak the same language. I was lucky because I spoke a few languages, so there was often one that was familiar. **(NOOR)**

As Diego describes, it can feel difficult if you are placed with carers who have a different ethnicity, as you can feel different, as if you stand out. He said that what helped him to feel accepted by his carers was that they said, 'You'll always be part of the family, whatever the colour of your skin.' He felt that this reassurance might help some young people, but other young people might not want to be part of someone else's family when they don't look the same, although it's always good to know that you will be accepted by them, no matter what.

How to plan a move

As a foster carer, you might not have a lot of say in how our moves are planned (especially if it's an 'emergency' or 'crisis' move), but it can help when we're asked questions and involved wherever possible. Asking what type of home or family we'd like to move to, or how we want the move to go, and giving us the chance to ask any questions first, can really help. We aren't asked enough about what we want, especially at times when there's so much change. In fact, some young people don't even know that they're going to move, or why, until the last minute (especially if they have a child protection plan). Please try to make sure that we know well in advance of any changes in our life, even if you think it will upset us, as it gives us a chance to say what we think, make some choices, and process what's happening. If not, it can feel like an even bigger jump for us to make.

As we described earlier, we might be on high alert, trying to read other people constantly to know if we're safe with them or not, and if we can trust them or not. Some of us have heard our foster carers talking about how much they have to do and how difficult it can be when we're moving in with them. We appreciate that it's a big change preparing for a new child to come into your home, but if we hear any hint of moaning or stress in your voice, it can make us fear the worst straight away – that you don't want us with you, that we're too much work, and that you'll give up on us quickly. So, it's important for us to know that you value us coming to live with you, that you want us there, and that you're committed to making it work.

Sometimes there might be a chance to do a 'graded' move, where we can talk to you, visit you, or meet you somewhere else first, and get to see and even decorate our new room. All these things are helpful. Please ask us what we want and would prefer, as we're all different, and will like and want different things. Asking us gives us some choice over something that we might feel no control over otherwise.

How we move is also important, as this can impact how scary and overwhelming it feels. Could there be an adult we know and feel comfortable with who takes us to our new home? This needs to be thought about carefully, as sometimes it can end up with people we don't know taking us to a new foster home, and sitting with us while we are trying to do this big, awkward, and very scary introduction.

It's important we have a chance to pack and think about what we want to take. Do you ever get the feeling that you've forgotten something just before going away on a trip? Imagine that feeling, while knowing you'll never be able to go back to get some of your most treasured possessions. Diego had to move in a hurry, and left all his toys, including a huge doll's house, behind. Lots of us have just been given bin bags or see-through plastic bags to pack, or only had the opportunity to pack a couple of things, meaning we've had to leave things that are important to us behind.

It would be bad enough as an adult if you were told one day that you were going to be staying briefly at a stranger's house, rather than going home. You would just say 'no' and choose to stay in a hotel instead. But if you're a traumatized child or young person, it's horrendous. This is not a choice, this move is usually forced, and you have no options about it.

Madlug was set up ten years ago. I was a youth worker and my wife and I were adoptive parents, and short-break foster carers. When we were going through an initial approval process, we were shown a video of a young girl talking about her belongings being put into a bin bag as she moved from one care placement to another. It made us think we wanted to do something about that. Our company provides bags to young people in care; every time we sell a bag, we give a bag too.

It's important to us that young people are treated with value, worth, and dignity. If we say that young people are valuable, then we need to treat them in this way. In our view, it's about giving them a proper bag that is theirs, and not something that you put rubbish into. Although people sometimes say that they use bin bags, or bags for life, to move their own things, they have the choice to do that. But young people don't always have that choice.

We are also aware that one of the main reasons why people use bin bags or carrier bags is that moves can often happen quickly – but that's even more of a reason to be prepared in advance and have a proper bag ready. We met with care-experienced children to think about what kind of bag they wanted, and what was important to them. They didn't want a branded bag due to stigma, so we offer a pack-away travel bag. The size of the bag also matters – if you give a young person too big a bag, it can reinforce the sense of having nothing (to fill it). So young people can have a number of these smaller bags if needed.

We've now given out 108,000 bags across the UK and Ireland. Our hope is that the bags also are a non-verbal communication of love and worth. We want every young person in care to know that we love, believe in them, and care about them. That's Madlug in a nutshell. (DAVE LINTON, FOUNDER OF MADLUG, *www.madlug.com*)

Tell us about yourselves

To start with, tell us a little about you and your family. Who are you and what are you like as people, and a family? What are your interests? What don't you like? What places do you like to visit? Do you have any funny stories to share? Any quirks? Who are your wider family and friends? Maybe share pictures with us.

As long as we're up to hearing it, sharing some information can help reduce that sense of 'the unknown' and prevent any wild stories we might concoct to fill in the gaps in our knowledge. This needn't be too formal, but something that helps us feel more familiar and safer with you can go a long way.

My carers told me stories about their family. Their older daughter was at university, and they introduced me to different family members by showing photographs and telling me about them, if they ever visited, and this definitely helped when visitors came. (SHANNON)

Share expectations

Another big thing that can help is if you can find a gentle way to let us know how you do things in your home and family, and what your expectations of us might be – but maybe try doing this naturally, rather than calling it 'house rules'. *This is how we do this, and this is how we do that.* What are the key things we might need to know about your home and ways of doing things? At the same time, be mindful that these ways of doing things might feel strange, uncomfortable, or difficult at first, particularly if it's a big change (e.g. being made to eat healthy food!). So pick your battles. For example, if we come into your house for the first time with our shoes on, remember that this is likely a really difficult time for us, and we might be experiencing lots of emotions, even if they're hidden. Please be kind, just let us sit down, and stay laid back about it. Addressing the shoes issues might feel as if a big barrier is being put in place, and it might make us worry about what things are going to be like, especially if we've never had to take our shoes off at home before (or if it feels safer to be wearing them, as they're ours). The shoe rule can always be talked about at a later time.

Let us know that you want us there

This might sound like an obvious thing, but when we first move in with you, we're likely to feel quite isolated and not part of your family. We might not feel that we fit in or as if we're wanted, so might choose to stay in our bedroom a lot of the time. We don't want to get in the way, and going downstairs to sit with you might feel quite intimidating at first.

> *Try to make time for your young person; try to get them out of their bedroom so that they can start to feel comfortable around you. Let them know that they're 'part of this family'. It can make a huge difference.* (AMY)

Invite us out to do activities with you, including family gatherings and meals, to let us know that you want us to be part of your family. We can always say 'no' if we don't feel that we want to, or if we're not ready to yet, but the invitation is valued.

> *When I first came to live with my carer, she would invite me out with her and her family. She would invite people round who would spend time with me, and wouldn't just go home because I was there. And she took me to the gym with her and taught me how to cook.* (DIEGO)

It can also help when you take an interest in whatever we're doing. So if we're drawing, maybe ask if we can draw together. Or it can be going for a drive somewhere together and having a chat along the way. Shared experiences don't have to be expensive or grand; they can be everyday things. Sometimes the smaller things can be more memorable than the bigger experiences. When you invest time in getting to know us and show that you want to spend time with us, then it lets us know that you care and that you're interested in us, which can make it easier for us to start to trust in you, and our relationship, over time.

Talk about names

When we first meet you, we might not know what to call you, or how to refer to you when we're talking to other people. Should we use your first name? Refer to you as our foster carer? Or call you something like Aunty? Cultural experiences can impact this too and can make it even more confusing for us to know what to call you. If this isn't agreed quickly, this can feel really awkward for us to ask about, as if the moment has passed. So it can be useful to have an early conversation: 'What do you want to call me? What should I call you? What feels comfortable?'

Make it informal

Sometimes the move can feel overly formal and difficult. We might have to be taken by social workers we don't know well, and sometimes we have to go to the social workers' office before going to our new home. Sometimes it can end up with us sitting with four 'big' unknown adults in the lounge of your home having a really awkward, uncomfortable conversation, wishing we could disappear and hide! The more informal the move can be, usually the better. Some ways you can make it a bit more informal are asking us if we want a drink or something to eat, letting us see our room or allowing us to spend some time settling in. It could be nice to sit down with us and have a little chat while we're unpacking our things, if we feel up to this. It can help to let us know that you're there if we need you, while also giving us some space.

Having our own bedroom helps as we have our own space, and that's important. If we want alone time, knock on the door, check on us, keep an eye on us without being intrusive. Let us have our own time to chill. We're in a new house, with a new family, so we feel isolated. Settling in is very important at that time. Being alone is how we adjust. A lot of young people will have fear of change so they need space to settle in, breathe, rest, and adjust to the house routine and what is going on. (DIEGO)

Take us shopping

Although it can be incredibly awkward at first walking round a supermarket with adults that we don't really know, it can actually help when you take us shopping soon after we first arrive. Often, we've had to pack our things quickly, and we might not have everything we need. We might have had to leave things behind too. It feels best when you let us have the chance to get both things that we need and things that we want, not just the absolute essentials. Having things we like and that are familiar to us can be a real comfort. It can be a bit of an icebreaker and something to do together at first. It's a way of getting to know what we like, which takes the pressure off a bit. It can also help us feel trusted and cared about and shows us that you want to make an effort with us.

I just felt they didn't try to interact enough, even if I was lashing out at the time. I stayed in my room a lot. There was no encouragement of games or asking what I wanted, or even a chance to talk about what I had been through. I also felt I didn't get a choice of personal hygiene products. I was just given pads, but I really would have preferred tampons, but I was too scared to ask. I suppose they weren't there to be my parents, but I had never experienced warmth, having meaningful chats. I also didn't feel very heard. I didn't get to choose any food or feel like I could ask for snacks and so on, even if it was to ask for some things I didn't like. I would have also really appreciated a bit more fun. All the walls were white, with a bed and drawers in the room. It sometimes felt as if I was in a hostel, more than a home. (JO)

Help us to feel part of the home

As described above, it's likely that we will experience your home at first as unfamiliar and different, belonging to someone else and not us. So it's important to make sure that we can start to feel that it's our home too. Sometimes having photos of us, our close family, or other people who are important to us up in the home can make us feel quickly part of it. But please ask us first! Or having things that are ours, such as items linked to our interests, out in the house, including the kitchen or living room, can make us feel more at home in those spaces. Then we don't feel that we always have to stay in our rooms, and we are okay being in other places in the house too.

If you can allow us to personalize our room, this can also be a powerful way of helping it to feel like our own. If not, it can feel as if we're staying in someone else's space. It's so important that we know our bedroom is really ours, and that the things we keep inside it are safe and won't be taken, disturbed, or moved. Please respect our property too – although it might look like nothing to you, it might be important to us or all we have that connects us to our past or particular memories or people. So, negotiating cleaning is a good step so that we know that you won't just be walking into our room to move things around without asking (which can feel very threatening). Sometimes our personal items are the only things that we've been able to keep as ours, while we've moved between homes, so we want to keep them safe and protected. Our bedroom needs to feel like a safe place that we can get away to. Talking through these things with us can be helpful, so that we all know what to expect, how our boundaries will be respected, and how things will be safe.

One thing that's very important is to identify what you're giving to us for us to keep (including when we move out), and what's for us just to borrow or use while we're living with you. It can be a horrible experience if we think that something (such as some new bedding that you bought when we moved in) is ours when you're wanting it back. We might become quite attached to these items and could feel rejected and possessive over them if you want to take them back from us when we weren't expecting it. It's important you name ownership of items early on so that we're both clear what's what.

Show us that you respect us

As young people in care, we'll have often had lots of experiences that might have led us to have to grow up quickly, be quite independent, and make decisions on our own. Sometimes we might have had to act like adults, looking after our siblings and even our parents. As mentioned above, older children may also feel that they need a house more than a family. If this is the case, moving into a new home with foster carers who set all the boundaries and rules can be difficult and frustrating, and there's a danger that we quickly feel patronized. Or when too many rules are stated straight away, this may even lead us to think, 'Well, now I don't want to do that!' When we're treated like young children, it can feel as if all the control and personal agency has suddenly been taken away, which feels scary, especially when we've been so used to having it. Instead, it can help when you sit down with us and we talk together about boundaries, expectations, and rules, letting us have some say. It can be a bit like contracting, and you can be quite creative with it, maybe writing things down or drawing out a bit of a mind-map and thinking together about what you both need. This can give a sense of ownership to us, is more likely to get us on board with the boundaries and rules, and, also, helps us to feel respected and as if you want to work with us. It can also help us to feel safer to ask questions that we could have been otherwise uncertain about asking you.

> *Personally, I found my carers actually getting to know me and my own personality and letting me come to them to discuss, share, reflect, or even just to talk, helped massively to develop the relationship. Looking back, I tried many different things to be understood and break down the barriers, but the thing that helped most was being seen and heard within the household, having my own decisions valued, and someone being there when things weren't okay.* (CJ)

We also know that sometimes you need to make decisions to keep us safe, even ones we might not like at the time. If you do need to make these decisions, please involve us in them as much as possible, and listen to us and try to understand our position too. Then please be honest and open with us and let us know why you've decided what you have, especially if it's against what we want. And let us know if it feels uncomfortable or tough for you too.

> *One of my carers wouldn't let me go out on my own for a long time, because of all the gangs I was involved in. I hated her for it, but it was helping me at the time to keep me safe. It was important that I could tell she was there and understood what I was going through and could tell I was scared even though I acted like I wasn't. It was how she was just there, and showed she would know what to do in situations, not panic or get scared – she'd know what to do and then act on it.* (DIEGO)

Consider mealtimes

It's important to think about mealtimes carefully, as these can be quite stressful at first. Every family or home does mealtimes differently, which can make it really confusing for us, as your mealtime traditions might clash with what we're used to. At first, it might feel hard for us to eat with your family. We might feel uncomfortable eating in front of strangers, might not be hungry at the same times (we could be used to different mealtimes, or be used to not eating for a while and then having a big meal), or might not like the food (it could be very different from what we're used to). It might be that we're used to eating separately in our room, so the idea of sitting at a table with a family can feel intimidating and very formal. Sometimes this may even lead us to want to miss meals completely or find ways to disrupt mealtimes. It can be useful to think with us about what our usual eating habits are, any dietary requirements or preferences, how we would usually do mealtimes, and what we tend to eat, and like to eat. It's also really important to take into account cultural differences.

I found it difficult to eat in front of people, as it caused a lot of anxiety and uncomfortableness. To help with this, the carers found that the best way to do this was to leave food with me and trust that I would return cutlery and plates back to the sink to be able to clean them. (CJ)

A good way to help to ease this potential stress is to include us in decisions about what we want to eat, presenting different options or even allowing us to cook for ourselves if we're old enough. Cooking together might be a nice option, if we want to do this, allowing us to show you what we usually eat. Please don't judge, even if this is quite different from what you're used to. If we are able to buy food and cook some of the meals that we're used to, this can help us to feel valued and more settled in the house, and as if you want to get to know us.

The power of pets

Animals are much less complicated than humans and can be really comforting and grounding, and a great talking point and distraction. It can help to have a focus when so much is going on. When you have a lot of new human relationships to navigate, spending time with a pet or animal can be comforting and uncomplicated because they just love us unconditionally, as we are. When Amy first moved into her foster home, she was surrounded by adults in the lounge, having to have really awkward conversations with people she didn't know yet. It was terrifying. Then her new carer's dog, Queenie, came over and sat on Amy's knee. Amy could then focus on Queenie, look at her, and cuddle her. She was really comforting, and she helped Amy to get through her first few days in her new home.

Of course, not all children like animals (they may be fearful of animals, have allergies, or there might be some risks), so please check this out before they move in. But if your child does, then visiting animals, or having pets in the house, can be a nice way of helping the child to settle in and experience some unconditional love and care.

The moving-in checklist

We've developed a moving-in checklist to help you to think about what you might want to consider before your new child moves in...

- Have we met you before we move in? Can we go for a walk together round the park, or maybe you could come and visit us at home first? Can we take it slowly?

- Pets – do you have them? Have you checked whether we like animals or have any allergies, whether we've had any pets previously, or whether there are certain rules around pets?

- Are you making sure you speak to us, the child, rather than the professionals in the room? This can be harder where professionals speak for us, but it can help if you keep involving us so that we don't feel pushed out.

- Start with a tour – 'This is the bathroom; this is where you sleep, where XXXX sleeps.'

- Think about how you'd like to spend time getting to know each other – you sharing a bit about yourself and your family, and asking us a little about us and our family. Keep this informal – it could be free-flowing conversation, or you could do a quiz or a game where you pick from different questions to answer, or prepare a little 'welcome pack', or swap photographs and spend time asking/answering questions about them.

- Can you take us shopping for clothes, toiletries, and other essentials we might need when living with you? Let us know whether we get to keep what we buy, or whether they will stay with you when we leave (this includes clothes!).

- Ask us about our preferences. What do we prefer to drink? What do we like for breakfast, dinner (and what do we call breakfast-lunch-dinner…or is it breakfast-dinner-tea!)? What time do we get up? What's our preferred routine? Just keep asking us lots of questions – this will help us build a relationship based on respect and trust. It can help us think, 'Oh they're asking me what I think; they must think what I want is important.'

- Are there things you expect from us? For example, anything we might think of as chores or rules? It's important to spell these out, as our expectations might be very different!

- Can you let us know about our own privacy – for example, will you go in our room?

- Consider where you will have private conversations, and make sure you don't have conversations outside these places. Remember that we have ears (even if we are 'asleep') and it only takes us overhearing one phone call for us to hear something we shouldn't.

- Think about your preconceived ideas – what are your views about our mum and dad or our situation? Don't share these with us, and don't let these views influence how you support us. Be curious with us about our own thoughts and feelings. Think about any assumptions you might have made about us and our life and be mindful of them; maybe challenge these assumptions by asking us about them.

- Is there anything you need to do to keep us safe, or anything you've been told you 'have' to do – for example, there might be rules around electronics?

Summary

Moving into a new home can be a terrifying, awkward experience with so much to learn and adapt to. If you can become aware of some of the challenges that we might face, you can find ways to help us feel more comfortable and as if we belong. Consider how to make your home's unsaid rules more transparent, talk with us about boundaries with some flexibility, and introduce us to your people, or pets or animals you might know, as this can all really help. Another big part of helping us to settle is starting to get to know us and what's important to us. We'll explore this more in the next chapter, when we think about how you can begin to understand us and hold our stories.

CHAPTER 3

Understanding Us and Our Stories

So we've moved into your home, and we are, essentially, strangers. You don't really know us aside from what you've read in reports or what other people have told you, and we don't really know you. As we talked about in the last chapter, at best, this can make things feel really awkward and difficult, and at worst, absolutely terrifying. When you show you want to get to know us, our life and stories, and you want us to get to know you and yours, it can make you seem safer, more familiar, and less of a mystery. It can make this weird situation feel easier for all of us.

When you're in care, there might be a lot to remember because so much changes all the time. We can get so caught up in navigating the day-to-day that sometimes we start to lose sight of our history, our journey, and our memories. When we have space to talk about our life, memories, and experiences, it helps us to remember and make sense of them.

In this chapter, we'll think about how you can get to know us more as a person and how this can help to deepen our relationship with you, and the importance of honouring and holding *all* our stories – including the positive and the mundane! We also think about how it's important to be led by us, at our pace and with care, when talking about more traumatic early experiences. We might not be ready to talk about this stuff yet, and that's okay too.

Help us to remember the good stuff

When we move into your home, it might make sense to just focus on the here and now or the future, because it's only from now on that we'll have shared experiences with you. Now we are in your life and your world, you'll want to do the best for us, and you might want to avoid stressing or upsetting us. This can mean that you might avoid asking us questions about our past, like who was important to us or in our life at crucial times. You might think that it's best not to focus on past relationships and worry that these could be tied up with some traumatic experiences or memories for us. But when people don't ask about our past because of the 'bad', it means that we don't get to talk about the 'good' either. There most probably will be positive things – good relationships that we've had with family members or friends, nice memories, things that we've achieved, or times with our family when things weren't as bad. If we avoid talking about the past completely, we don't have the chance to remember and reminisce about the normal, everyday good stuff as we would if we were growing up with our own family.

> *When we have the opportunity to share memories with you, reminisce, and talk about past experiences and relationships (even if you were not a part of them), this can be important to us.* (CJ)

Routines, rituals, traditions

Rather than assuming that we'll fully adjust to your lifestyle as it is, perhaps instead, think about how you can learn more about us and what's important to us, and try to merge your life and ours. What things could we do together that would be important for both of us? What things are part of your lifestyle that you would love us to get involved with? But also, what traditions, routines, rituals, experiences are ours that we might want to continue? And are there any of these that we might want to bring you into, or that you could support us with? What new traditions could we start together? How could you help us to feel incorporated and part of your life, so that it starts to feel like our home too?

Knowing what's important to us and our journey can also help you to know what might help us to feel more settled in our home with you. For example, if we have always had a tradition of going to church on a Sunday, and getting an ice-cream on the way home, then offering us the chance to continue with this tradition if we wish to can make things feel more normal and familiar, which can help us feel that life is more predictable and safer. It also shows that you value getting to know us and what's important to us. So try to understand a bit more about the good and the mundane from our past too, and see what you can keep going.

The stories we share with you may highlight lots of our positive qualities, strengths, and resources – whether we know it or not! For example, our fierce independence, our problem-solving skills, tenacity, our great empathy and love for our brother, the strength we showed when getting through a particularly difficult time, or our skills and love for baking, art, music, sport, or caring for others.

Our people

There might be people who were really important to us growing up who we've lost contact with through being in care, and the many changes that we have gone through. We might be missing our family or past carers, friends, teachers, social workers, or therapists. Sometimes we may have lost contact but might not ever have been told why we can't see or speak to these important people any more. It's likely that, as a foster carer, sometimes you might not even be told who was important to us, why they were important, or what we remember about them and our relationship to them. You could easily form an opinion of that person if you are given specific information about them from, say, a social care file, but you won't really know how we experienced our relationship with them or what that was like. We might see things differently from how they've been documented.

It might be that there is an auntie we really love spending time with, who has been there for us throughout our lives, and with whom we have happy memories. Having a better understanding of this relationship and how important it is to us can mean that you try to prioritize it for us, making sure we have opportunities to see our auntie and do things that we really enjoy with her. This could include, where possible, upholding traditions that we might have, such as a phone call at a weekend or seeing each other at Easter.

See Chapter 4, where we think about the importance of our relationships and networks and how to keep these going or even build on them.

Hold our story

The more moves we have, the harder it can be for us to keep a sense of who we are and what's happened in our lives. If we've had lots of changes in professionals too, it can feel as if no one is keeping a full record of what has happened, what we have been through (the good and bad), and who has been alongside us through these journeys – no one is 'holding our stories'. Most young people will have their journeys and stories held by their parents, families, and friends through talking about shared memories and collating photos and important items along the way.

Also, there can often be lots of things happening all at once, and it can be hard for us to remember and hold on to what's happened, which means that big chunks of our life can sometimes be forgotten. It's also important that we find ways to talk about our life before. It's part of who we are and not talking about it can leave us feeling that we're denying it. This can lead to us 'compartmentalizing' or putting our past in a box, denying or trying to ignore parts of who we are.

At the same time, it can feel as if everyone already knows our history, because of how little control we have over how our information is stored and where it's shared, which can feel horrible and exposing. It's our life, so it's hard knowing all that personal information has to be shared with everyone. We can end up feeling as if nothing is private. But it's important you know what's happened to us, so you can understand us better.

We recognize that it can be scary to talk to us about our early life. You might be afraid to say the wrong thing or make things worse. You might feel scared to open up 'Pandora's box'. You might be worried about telling us that you know things that we don't think you know. But it can help having space and time to talk things through with you if we want to, as long as it's led by us because we want to talk, rather than led by you because *you think* it will help us to talk.

> *When you're in care, it's important to have environments where you can feel safe to talk about your life and what you've been through. My foster carer was a nosey person so he would always ask me, and I never got that with other carers. It was like they didn't care about what happened before. Having a deep conversation is valuable. But sometimes he would ask me at funny times, I was like, 'Pick your moments XX, don't ask me on the way to school.' Carers might feel some kids are hard to crack, but then you just ask them, and they will tell you everything. They will tell you or let you know if they don't want to. As a child, you don't even know how to understand what you've been through so it might be hard to talk. Maybe they could just acknowledge what you've been through, and that they are there to talk about it, if you want. They [carers or professionals] never even told me why I was in care. It's like they don't want you to know your own past and what you've been through, but it is your life.* (ANGEL)

How to talk about our past

When we feel ready to talk to you about what's happened to us in the past, it can be helpful to give us the space and time to do this at our own pace. Let us have a voice in telling our own story or journey, because who knows us better than ourselves? There'll likely be things that we'll know about ourselves that others, including professionals, won't know. These conversations may feel awkward, but the important thing is your approach and your intention.

For you to gain a well-informed understanding, it's important for you to speak to other people who know us well too, such as our past carers, professionals who've worked with us, teachers in our school, or our families. Although we might be able to tell you some things about our past, we might not be able to remember everything and there might be things that we're not fully aware of or didn't understand at the time, or we might not be able to articulate what's happened. This is particularly true if we've experienced trauma in our early life, which can massively impact our recollections. We might not remember what happened, we might have gaps in our memory or fragmented memories, or we might not know or understand what happened.

In the beginning, my foster family felt they had to be careful what they asked and what to do with it, because they had a kid that had come over the sea [as a refugee], and people didn't know my story. And they might ask and know where you're from, but not understand what it means. There was a lot of trauma. I had seen people die. So you have to be careful. They would ask questions when they could see I was comfortable to talk. Once they knew more about me, they could support me to contact my family and go to the mosque with other Muslim people. People assumed because I wear hijab, and I was at university, that I was from a well-educated family and they were shocked when I said, 'I'm a refugee'. When you have been through that journey, you are so proud of what you did. So when people say 'poor you', or look at you with empathy, I think it dismisses all the achievements of what I went through. I don't want to feel I am weak or to be looked at as weak. It was not a nice journey, with horrible situations and conditions, but it wasn't bad, as it made me who I am. (NOOR)

Really hearing and understanding what we decide to share with you is important. Whatever information we choose to talk about, whatever memories we want to discuss, can be important 'clues' in being able to understand us better, so it's important to hold these in mind. When you understand our history, it can help you to know more about who we are as a person, what the meaning might be behind some of what we do (e.g. why we might fear getting close to others because in the past when we got close, people left or we got hurt), what we might need, and how you can help and support us to feel safe.

It's crucial to think about the intention of your conversation. It's not okay to go 'digging' for information about the traumas that we've been through, as this can be unhelpful or even re-traumatizing for us. If we want to talk about something, we'll tell you in our own time.

How our past impacts us

It's important to think about how our past might be impacting our behaviour, our actions, our words. Be curious about what you see – what's leading us to act in this way? What might be underneath our behaviour? For example, could we be feeling rejected, or fearful of being hurt?

> *There were a lot of things from my past that were not necessarily addressed, and had my foster carer known, and had the type of relationship with me where she had understood me better, she might have known what kind of support I needed.* (KIM)

There's a danger that if you don't understand our history and what we've been through, you might think that we're 'acting out' or misbehaving, which could lead you to tell us off or become frustrated with us, rather than recognizing that it might be a cry for help. We recommend that all foster carers undergo training that helps them to understand how trauma can impact a young person's development, even into adulthood, the different ways in which trauma can manifest itself in how the young person copes and acts, and how they, as a foster carer, can help. If things from our early history haven't been understood, or we've not had the right kind of support or treatment, these things may still affect us as an adult. You might see patterns of things that were happening for us when we were a child still playing out today, if we've not had the opportunity to process and move on from them. If you know and understand our history, it gives you the chance to act accordingly, and make sure that you're supporting us in the best way possible and meeting our underlying needs.

Talking about our past experiences, our family, friends, rituals, routines, and even the very big stuff, can help us to make sense of our experiences, and thoughts and feelings about them, and sort them into our memory bank. It can help us to normalize, make sense of, and contextualize what happened to us, which can enable us to understand our past as a range of experiences separate from us, rather than us becoming defined by our past.

When we move into your home, away from the possibly traumatic or chaotic environment that we've come from (whether we've moved from our family home, another foster home, or residential care), it might be that we start to feel that things are a bit calmer, and we have more space to think. This can mean that our mind can go back to the past, because we then have some thinking space, and we might start to reflect on the things that we've gone through and what has led to us living in your home.

Once I'd settled into my foster placement, I developed an eating disorder. This had never been something I had noticed until this time, and it was a shock to me and my foster carers. When I think back on it now, I believe it was due to my negative experiences at home that I had linked with food, but it took me being settled into what I felt was a safe space before this trauma began to show itself. (MIA)

This settled time once we've moved in with you, however, can also be a time when people are actively trying not to talk about the past with us, as they might not want to distress us further, but this can feel really hard. It can then feel as if no one is noticing or caring what we're going through, or even as if part of our life has been swept under the rug.

Tips for talking about our stories

Here are a few things to consider before talking to us about our early history:

- It's important to navigate these conversations really carefully, and not just jump in with direct questions. Take time to think about how best to do this and what we might need.
- Create a safe space to have these conversations, ideally away from your home; for example, going on a walk to a favourite place together or going for a drive in the car – somewhere we can feel safe and comfortable to talk.
- When having these types of conversations, we need to be able to get away if it feels too much – to know that we can leave and walk away, to find some space to feel okay again.
- We would recommend that these types of conversations are not had in places like our bedroom. If the conversation becomes quite upsetting or triggering, and it's being held within our bedroom, that could lead to our bedroom no longer feeling like a safe space. Being there could remind us of that conversation and not feeling like we can leave.

'I'm not ready to talk yet'

We might not feel able to share our experiences with you, especially at first. It's the fear of the unknown. Once we share something with you (or someone else), it's out there in the open and we're powerless to take it back. We might worry about the potential implications of what we've said (lots of us will have been taken into care because of what we've shared in the past). We might worry about where the information will go (and whether it'll be written down somewhere), who it will be shared with, and what might happen (how what we've shared might impact other people). This makes it really tough for us to know whether we should share or not.

Even if we react in a way that seems to be shutting you down at first, this doesn't necessarily mean that we don't want to talk about our life before at all. It might just mean that it's not the right time, that we feel caught off guard, or that we aren't quite ready to talk about it yet. Or we might want to talk, just not about 'that'. Sometimes it might feel easier for us to say 'shut up' rather than explaining why we're not ready. So pacing it, giving opportunities for us to talk, and being gently curious with us, while also listening to what we tell you, are all important.

Some of us might have grown up being told that bad things would happen if we shared what was happening at home. Or we might have been told that things at home should stay private and are 'family matters', or that people would never believe us if we did say what was happening. Some of us may have even shared things before, but then been ignored, dismissed, not believed, or blamed, so why would we bother sharing something so personal again?

It takes a good rapport and trust for us to feel safe to open up to you. It takes time to build this, before you can start to ask us about ourselves more deeply. If we're still strangers and we've only had limited, surface level conversations, then it can feel way too much to be asked about our history, or what we might carry with us day-to-day. It's more likely that we would close up to protect ourselves and not want to speak. It's a lot to ask of us. It's important that we can tell you things in our own time. It's okay for us to not be ready yet.

> *I personally feel very much like I was hiding it, and maybe that's because I didn't really want to talk about it at the time, and I didn't really want to deal with it, because it was in the forefront of my mind, and I was still coming out of that situation.* (CJ)

We might feel comfortable to say things occasionally and to share a little information, but might not want to go further, or we might want to take things at our own pace. It's important to respect that. You can let us know that you're there if we want to talk about anything but let us take the lead. You can say, 'When you're ready to speak about anything, you can come to me', and then create opportunities for us to be in safe spaces to enable us to talk when, and if, we're ready to. Sometimes it might help if we went for a walk, or a drive, or did an activity together while talking. It can also be helpful, especially if it seems as if we want to tell you something but we aren't quite sure yet, to ask us what we might need to feel safe to speak. It might be that there is something getting in the way (e.g. a fear or uncertainty) that we can share with you.

But some of us still might not be ready or want to talk (even after we've left care), and that's still okay. This might feel frustrating to you at times, and you might wish that you could be having these conversations with us. But we might not feel able to yet, so it's important that you understand and accept this.

Be transparent about sharing

For us to feel okay sharing, we need to know what'll happen to the information we share, what you'll be able to keep private (realistically), and what you would need to share more widely (and to whom, and how it would be shared). It's incredibly important that you don't make false promises, as you can't ever give us a guarantee that you won't share something with anyone else. If our life, or someone else's, is at risk, or someone is at risk of serious harm, you'd need to share the information to keep people safe. You don't want to have to breach that trust if we believe that *everything* we share is safe with you. This is so hard, as children who aren't in care don't have to worry about these things in the same way; it's unlikely that their parent would need to share things with other people, or that this information would be written down permanently in a care record.

This can be difficult – you're trying to provide a home, care, and love to us, while also needing to keep us and others safe, and share risky information when you need to. But please don't ambush us by speaking to a social worker about something we've shared and then have them turn up to discuss this with us. This makes us want to hide information and it damages our relationship with you. So, being as transparent and open as possible is important to help us trust in you and learn that you will do what you say you will.

The challenges of accessing files

Although we might have some knowledge about our past, it might be that we don't remember everything. Or it might be that we don't really understand what happened to us. A lot of our history will be written down in our social care file, which we probably won't get to see until we are 18 years old, and only then if we request to see it. Sometimes what's written down in our file can be incorrect, labelling, hard to read, or just full of professional jargon. Although sometimes you might think that it is best to just give us a copy of our previous reports, so that you're being open and transparent with us, please don't do that without thinking it through first, and considering how we might experience reading through it.

> *It's like they're describing a kidnapped victim. They will say, 'tall, slim build', stuff like that. They describe you based on physical appearance and then what you are doing. If you don't have a hobby, then they make a big deal about it. They tried to force me into so many activities I didn't want to do. It feels like you're an experiment, like in a research project. You don't feel like you're being seen. It's just words they write, and you just end up feeling that there is a lack of effort or care. The language is repetitive and robotic. It's not personalized and it's so generalized they could be talking about anyone.* **(ANGEL)**

Also, please think about what you write down about us or talk about in meetings concerning us. You'll be influencing what's written about us, and how, too.

Some of the words and phrases that we particularly dislike include, 'challenging behaviours', 'naughty', 'difficult child', and when our choices are labelled 'silly' or 'naïve'. These words are so judgemental and don't provide any understanding about what we've been through or why we might be acting in this way. Once someone uses a word like this, it might fuel the fire of how other people think about us too.

It's also important to think about how it's written down. Years later, the child might not be in that place any more. They might have done something one time when they were six years old, but professionals carry that story on with them once it's written down, shared, and described in a particular way. Imagine being reminded of the worst thing that you've ever done, again and again, even when it was years ago, and you've moved on in your life.

When we turn 18, we might want to access our file to find out more about our history, and it can be useful for us to get some support to read and digest what's written about us and our family. Sometimes social care departments offer support, but it can help if you're able to offer to help us with it too, especially if we have a strong bond. It's likely that we might want to find out more about the reasons why we ended up in care, or the reasons why we couldn't see, or live with, particular relatives. Or it might be that we have vague memories about something, and we want to know what really happened.

Informal 'life story work'

Life story work can vary from young person to young person. It can be quite formal (such as developing a life story book with a 'professional' of some sort, or writing/drawing out a timeline) or it can just be about having information about your past available if you want to look at it, or talking it through with someone with whom you feel safe.

> *Life story work didn't hold much significance for me during my time in care, other than a few trips to visit the hospital where I was born and a shiny book to share with people who wanted to understand my story. I grew tired of verbally sharing it repeatedly. My life story work was done over two weeks when I was 12, and then there was nothing until I took responsibility for it as an adult.*
>
> *Now, as a 37-year-old care-experienced professional*

and mother of two, life story work means something entirely different to me. I wish that the intense two-week period at the age of 12 had started when I first entered care at the age of five and continued throughout my time in care. Life story work, or as I prefer to call it, memory collation, forms the foundations of your identity. Without an identity, you can easily get lost in a social care system that wants to assign labels and put you in boxes for the sake of process and procedure.

I realize now how damaging a lack of memories can be for anyone, not just young people in the care system, especially as I navigate motherhood. My focus for my children is to capture everyday moments through collating pictures, stories, videos, school reports, favourite items of clothing, and toys. Most importantly, I want to capture everyday moments by spending time talking and reflecting with them, usually at bedtime when they are most willing to chat with Mum and Dad in hopes of staying up for an extra 15 minutes. These moments of reflection help to cement those everyday memories so they are stored not just in a physical form but in their hearts and minds too.

Our experiences shape us into the people we are and guide how we navigate the complexity of relationships, whether with our children, friends, or colleagues. The lack of everyday memories from my childhood motivates me to do better for my children, ensuring that when they are 37, they know what their favourite colour was in primary school, who their first best friend was, how old they were when they first wore lipstick or had their ears pierced.

My hope for the future is that the trusted adults around children in care and leaving care appreciate the importance of collating everyday memories for and on behalf of the children they look after. By openly demonstrating the significance of these everyday memories, they can help children and young people start to create an identity of which they can be proud of and which becomes part of their narrative now and in their future. (ROSIE)

For some young people, having a life story book, which talks about both the good things and the bad, and the mundane, can be really anchoring. This life story book is usually created by our social worker, but we might sometimes want to talk through it with you. It's important that this is led by us, and if we don't want to look at it, that's fine too.

Life story books can often feel easier to look at than our full social care record, as if we get access to our records, they're made up of thousands of pieces of paper; half of them can be redacted or poorly written, and they don't tend to make us feel good about ourselves. They can also portray a negatively skewed picture of our life too, focused on 'problems' rather than any of the good parts. So, having a life story book which talks through the good stuff too, and helps us to understand the different things that have happened, can help. But it's important that we've chosen to go through it. We might also have support from other professionals to go through our life story sometimes, as talking through it can be really difficult or upsetting for some of us, especially if we don't remember it all.

For other young people, we might want to have the opportunity to keep memories through scrapbooks, memory boxes, or photos, including of our time with you. This could help us to talk about stories together and share memories. It's also really important that this is led by the young person, as we all might want different things. However, it would be lovely for you to collect things for us as memories that you can keep. Then if we see you again in the future, you have memories and things that remind you of us and our time together, which you can get out to show us. Please use your common sense and compassion about what to keep, and make sure that it's only about good things.

Be aware of our readiness

When sharing information with us, it's really important to think about our context, age, and readiness to hear the information.

Sometimes we might have a lot of vulnerability around particular relationships, or have lots of trauma memories that could be easily triggered by a discussion about the past. Try to balance the importance of sharing information with thinking about whether this is the right time to share it with us as an individual. And whether it would serve us any purpose or benefit right now, or whether it would be more beneficial for us to find out later in life, when things are more settled for us. This is particularly the case, for example, if we are going through a big change, or we have lots of stressful things happening, and giving us distressing information at that point would potentially be really unhelpful.

So before you share information with us about our past that we might not know, consider the following points:

- Have a think with other people supporting us about whether it's the right time for us to know, or whether it wouldn't be beneficial for us right now, and if it would be better to leave it until a later date, when things are more settled, or we have more trusting relationships to support us.

- Who is the best person to have this conversation with us? Do you have a relationship with us that feels safe and trusting enough at this stage? (This trusting, safe relationship is the bedrock before any difficult conversations can be had.)

- If you're going to be talking to us, make sure that you've thought about what you'll say and how. Make sure that you have the information you need to answer any questions we might have. For example, it wouldn't be helpful to tell us that our parent is unwell, without being able to answer further questions around this.

- Think about what we might need to support us around this conversation – when would you tell us, what do we have on that day/week, who will be around to support us and how, where could the conversation be that would help us to feel safe?

The problems with missing information

Sometimes when we don't know why a decision was made, such as why we're not able to see a particular family member, it can lead to understandable uncertainty, resentment, and frustration. We may feel angry at the people who made the decision to stop us seeing our family member, or may direct this emotion at you as our carer. We may feel resentment or upset at the family member, assuming that they've done something to prevent them being able to see us, or we may feel rejected or abandoned by them. This could then lead to a breakdown in that relationship, even if this was an important relationship for us, and one that could have been safe and rebuilt in the future (even if this is when we're an adult). This could also lead to us doing things that could be seen as risky (such as hitchhiking or running away) to see that family member, if we don't understand why we shouldn't see them, or feel that people are keeping us away from them. The lack of communication or transparency around this could be a real problem for us and our family.

Humans tend to 'fill in the blanks' when they don't fully know information, and to make their best guesses as to what's happened – but sometimes we can get this completely wrong, which will impact what we choose to do. For example, we may have an understanding that we were taken away from our family and placed in care due to our family 'neglecting' us, as this is what we'd heard from our social worker or other professionals. From this description, we may start to build up a picture that our family didn't care about us at all, didn't look after us, and, in essence, rejected us. What we might not be aware of is that our mum tried her best to look after us, but really struggled to do this due to her alcohol dependency. Mum also had her own difficult childhood and history of trauma, and drinking alcohol was how she blocked out all the bad memories. At times, perhaps Mum was able to take care of us, and professionals were able to see how much we were loved and well cared for. But when Mum was struggling, she found it hard to keep us safe. Our mum may have fought to try to keep us in her own care, but the court decided that she was unable to consistently care for us safely, which may have led to us being taken into care.

Summary

It can be really powerful if you are able to support us to understand our story, if and when we're ready to do this. Some of us may have moved so many times within our lives that it could be hard for us to hold on to a narrative about what's happened and where we've been, and who's been around us. When talking to us about the past, it's important to pace this, let us lead, and allow us to share stories (the good stuff and the mundane, as well as the not so good). This also helps us to hold on to stories and memories about ourselves, our lives, and people who were, and still are, important to us. In the next chapter, we think about the importance of our relationships and connections throughout our lives.

CHAPTER 4

Building Relationships and Networks

When you're in care, you often move around a lot, whether it's moving home, between family members, moving school, moving social workers, or moving to a completely different area, sometimes far away. Moving to one respite carer, then to another, and another. Moving GPs, dentists, youth clubs, moving between friend groups...the list just goes on. Moving might be good sometimes; you can meet new people and have new and different experiences. But it also might mean that you leave your important people, places, and communities. Moving, leaving, and losing people can leave us feeling left behind, alone, and isolated. And sometimes our relationships can end badly or feel fractured. It hurts to lose people we care about.

Relationships are everything when you're a young person in care. You need your people, especially when you leave the care system behind. Technically, at that point, you have no one apart from your family, and that's only if you still have contact with them. It can feel ironic to need your family so much after years of being protected from them, particularly when for some of us, there have been periods when we've not been allowed to see them.

When you're taking a child from their family home into a new environment, despite all the focus on the here-and-now, it's important not to forget about what, and who, was important to them in the past. When we have positive relationships, or at least ones that we wish to maintain with people who have been with us throughout our lives, then we could be thinking about them a lot and missing these people. It might feel that no one seems to really notice what we're going through or care about it. It can also seem as if there's a part of our life that has been just forgotten about and has to be swept under the rug. So if you can show an interest in, and be curious with your child about, their key relationships, this can be really powerful.

In this chapter, we explore how you, as a foster carer, can help us to stay connected in our relationships – even the tricky ones – and support us to build bigger networks.

Why relationships are so important to us

As so much is in flux when you're living in care, often it's just the few stable relationships you have (if you've been able to make and keep them) that remain the same. They can feel like anchors, or pillars, helping us stay grounded and holding the rest of our life up when so much is constantly changing, uncertain, or difficult. It's important that we're given the chance to build supportive relationships that can stay with us for life.

> *I remember the day before Christmas, I was just on campus [at university] by myself. My friend's mum called me and was like, 'Kim, come, don't stay at uni by yourself.' So it was nice to have those networks. And that's why I say that when you're in care, you really need to build networks outside the care system because those are the people who are with you for life. I think the care system will have you up to 18, 21, and 25, those key ages. Then it eventually leaves you and those networks that you built outside the system are what carry you. I've been so lucky that I've never spent a Christmas by myself since I left care. I've always had my friend's family to go to, and my church family, who have always been there to kind of help me.* (KIM)

Loneliness

Another big challenge is loneliness, which can be a huge thing for us. We might not notice it at first, if we're used to being alone. But then loneliness can creep in. When you're used to losing people because you're moving around so much, trusting in your relationships can be hard, even the new ones. *Why would I bother trying to build a relationship with you if I'm only going to be moving on again?* Some of us can also feel quite different from other young people, who are just going through everyday stresses when we're going through very difficult challenges related to being in care. We might distance ourselves, because how can other people relate to or understand this kind of stress? It can feel isolating and all of a sudden, you're alone and lonely with it. You need a bit of a push and some support to connect with people, even when it's hard.

Talk about our 'support networks' with us

Often it's assumed that we *must* have some people to support us somewhere. Social workers often ask, 'Who's in your support network?' with an assumption that there will be someone there if we really look hard. But sometimes we might have literally no one on whom we can lean for support during hard times. When we don't have people around and we don't have that option, there's no back-up plan. This is scary, so often we just learn to get on with things ourselves.

> *I was really lucky to have the same PA [personal advisor] for around nine years of my life, and with little contact with my biological family, I often felt that she was the only consistent person in my life. Some years, hers was the only Christmas card or birthday card I received. When I turned 25, I had to say goodbye to her as she was no longer my PA and at the time I felt completely abandoned and alone. When I look back now, I really wish that those support networks had been encouraged and supported because there are times even now when I struggle, as we all do in life, and I find myself completely alone.* (MIA)

Make positive relationships a focus

We strongly believe that relationships and networks should be on the agenda from when we first enter the care system, throughout our time in care, to when thinking carefully about preparing us to leave care and making future plans. It should be an absolute priority. You, as our foster carer, can start to talk to us about this right from the beginning. It's important for you to know who's in our life, and who we want to be there. Even if you don't think they are 'good' for us, they might be all we have, and we need someone!

Here are some ideas of things to think about with us:

- Who are the people in our lives that we value and want to stay in our lives? How can we build these relationships or make them feel steadier and more consistent? (This might mean we see people less but the quality of our time together is better.)

- Who do we go to if we need something? Or if we want to talk? Or if we want to feel close to someone? Or have fun? (These might be different people.)

- Who have we felt closest to in our lives? What have those relationships felt like?

- Is there anyone we want to be closer to? Are there any relationships that are hard, damaged, or even broken? How can we work towards rebuilding these (even if this is a long-term fix)?

- Are there relationships that leave us feeling bad about ourselves, or that keep us feeling stuck? Any that even feel toxic for us? What do we see as the problems in these relationships?

- What other kinds of relationships do we think we might be missing? Are there any that we want more of? Or want to deepen?
- What might get in the way of us getting close to people and building solid relationships with them?
- What networks or communities are we involved in, or have we been involved in in the past? Can we reconnect with these (e.g. church, football team, band, clubs at school)?

It's good to think about the relationships that are working well, as well as the ones that aren't. For example, it could be that we have a difficult relationship with our sister, but no one has really picked up on that before and we want this to change. You might be able to support us to build this relationship gradually, so that by the time we leave care, we have a family member that we are closer to, who will be with us during our adult life when you're not. If not, it could mean our relationship continues to deteriorate, and we end up with even less family around us in the future.

Strengthen existing relationships

When you know our important people, you can then help to find opportunities for us to see them and strengthen those relationships. For example, you might support us to visit our sister once a fortnight or stay over occasionally at a friend's house. It might be that you support us to arrange video calls, or other ways to stay in touch, if we aren't able to see each other in person.

It might help to start small and build up the time we spend together, to see how we find it. Are we enjoying spending time with that person? Does it feel too much? What do we like about it? What don't we like? Can we do something different to help it feel easier? It might feel complicated too, because relationships are complex, let's face it! We might like spending time with that person *and* find it a bit too much. With this, it might help to build in some ways to take a break or leave early, or have some quiet down time scheduled in for after we see them (this might be for an hour or a couple of days, depending on how it feels).

Please don't stop us from seeing people we want to see, just because it's hard – because not seeing your important people is worse than feeling bad for a bit after you've seen them.

There can also be people that we're missing because they've died, maybe even while we've been in care. This can feel especially tough, if they were someone that we felt close to, and we didn't get to see as much of them as we wanted. We might want your help to find a way to remember or celebrate the loved ones we've lost.

Explore family relationships

Family relationships can be essential to us, as our families are usually a big part of our identity, our story, and our sense of who we are. So we think that those around us, such as our foster family, should work hard to help us to keep these relationships going.

> *As a young person, I was like no, absolutely not [seeing family]. But no one tried pushing me back. At the time, I was 14, so I probably could have done with some further support for them and me around this to see if a relationship could have been built again.* (MIA)

Sometimes we might not be able to see the bigger picture or other perspectives at the time and might only see what's in front of us.

It's helpful when you can be curious and explore things with us to help us to see other potential points of view.

When CJ left his family home, he wished that someone had asked him about his sister and where she lived, and showed they were curious about her. It can be helpful when you can be curious about our life before, but in a gentle, graceful way. It gives us the option of talking about what we want to, but without pressure, and gives you an opportunity to find out what, and who, is important to us.

It's also crucial to understand the context. It might seem, or be written down in the notes, that we don't get on with our brother, for example. It might be that we've been fighting for years, and in the end, we couldn't live together in foster care. But there might have been context during this time we were living together – maybe we were both struggling to adapt to living in care, or with the rules set out in our new foster home, and missing our family and the area where we grew up. So, maybe we were taking it out on the person we felt closest to (our brother), or maybe we were angry at him because we thought that it was his fault we ended up in care. Giving us a bit of space to talk about our relationships and what's happened can be really helpful, as it's only with that space that we (and you) can start to make sense of what might have got in the way of these relationships, and what led them to break down. And then we can decide if we want to work on repairing these relationships, and how.

Being separated from my siblings was done in such a traumatic way. They didn't tell us, and my brother said, 'Oh, I'm staying back [from school] for the day.' We all went to school and came back, and he was gone; all his things were gone. He wasn't told he was moving either. I don't think they thought they had to tell him until the day he was actually going. And then they moved him far away and his behaviour got worse after that as well. It was all really bad. (ANGEL)

On the flip side, we might feel there is pressure or expectation for us to see a certain person too. Asking us questions, being curious about what we say in a genuine attempt to understand what we might be thinking and feeling (without having your own agenda), and giving us choices about how to navigate these situations can really help. Reassure us that we can take them at our own pace, and try to plan and structure things in advance, as that helps too.

Sometimes we aren't always asked who we want to see, and there can be an expectation that we want to see our family members. The meet-ups can just be decided by adults in our lives and booked in, and we might feel that we just have to go along with them, sometimes with very little or no preparation. Some relationships in our lives might feel particularly difficult, upsetting, and even scary. This might be seeing the person who was abusive to us or someone else in our family, or someone who reminds us of what happened at home, so seeing them could bring up big feelings and memories and feel re-traumatizing (as if we're back there again). It might be that we really don't want to see this person, but we feel that we have to and have no control over it. Or it might be that we find it hard to let people know how we're feeling about seeing them, thinking people will judge us or ignore what we say (e.g. people might think that of course we want to see this person, or we *should* see them, because they're family). Please don't decide for us without giving us space to talk things through. Ask how we're feeling about the person and how it feels seeing them, if we want to see them or not, or if there's anything we need to think about to make it easier seeing them, as all these prompts can help us to feel as if you'll listen and respect our views and make it easier for us to speak up.

Sometimes it can get complicated in other ways. We might desperately want to see someone, but there might be restrictions in place, or it might be that even if there aren't, we feel that we're being prevented from seeing them. If we feel that we are being stopped from seeing our people, then we might find our own ways to go and see them, which could be unsafe (such as getting on a train alone when we're not old enough to do this safely, or not telling you where we're going). Please understand that if we're feeling really alone and are missing the people who are important to us, this might feel like the only way. And don't forget that we might be used to being by ourselves, or travelling alone, even if this is something that you don't think that we should be doing (we might not see the problem). But safety should always come first. This is another reason why open conversations about relationships and who's important to us, and working out safe ways in which we can keep in contact, are important.

I wasn't allowed to see my mum and I hadn't seen her for about three years. I knew she wasn't well enough to look after us, but I didn't know why I couldn't see her – because I knew she was a good person, but people would insinuate she was not a good person because they wouldn't let me see her. I really missed my mum. We got in touch over Facebook, and I arranged to meet her at McDonald's after a class I had after school. I was so excited and I had such a good time. Then I got back, and my friend's foster carer rang me and said they would tell my foster mum, unless I told her first. She gave me two hours and she seemed so angry, so I felt like I had done a bad thing. It's your instinct to see your mum. I would cry about not seeing her, so of course I'd take the chance to see her. She's my mum! I wouldn't have changed anything or undone it, but it put my brain into turmoil. I was going to get in the worst trouble. And I didn't even know what to say. My foster carer was so lovely about it. She just sat next to me on the bed and said, 'How was it?' and I said, 'It was amazing' and she said, 'That's great. Obviously, you can't do it again, but I'm glad you had a nice time and you're safe, everything is fine.' And I was so shocked she reacted that way as the other foster carer was so angry about it and I thought it was so bad and that I was going to get in so much trouble. I know that a lot of foster kids would sneak out and see their family, because it's so important to them, and they don't understand why they can't. It's almost like that gets in the way of everything else, not seeing their family when they want to. (ANGEL)

Support us to rebuild relationships

As we've described already in this chapter, having long-term relationships is so important, whether these are with family, friends, or other people within our wider communities. When the care system leaves us, our long-term relationships and networks will be all we have.

If we have broken relationships while we're in care, the odds of these relationships being magically rebuilt, without any support, are probably slim to none. As anyone does, we need to be able to work through any challenges, and have the chance to repair and re-invest in the relationships we have. Sometimes people think that relationships that have broken down (such as with our parents) can be left until we leave care, and instead relationships in the here-and-now should be prioritized, which might make sense. However, when we've left care, it can be so much harder to try to reconnect with people and rebuild relationships. At this stage, there are often so many different things to navigate as we start living more independently. But also, so much time will have passed, so the desire to try to fix those relationships may be long gone. It might be that we've lived with feelings of upset or resentment over time, or the words and actions that were previously expressed may have created a lot of built-up hurt, so we no longer want to try to reconnect with that person.

> *When I was in and out of care, I was always going back to my mum. My social workers were really good at supporting that relationship, realizing the importance of it. It felt like they taught my mum to love. It was really special and I really valued that. Despite entering and re-entering care 14 times, I knew I was loved and I had a sense of family because of that. Quite a lot of children in care end up going home to their families, so we need to support that relationship as much as possible. Quite a lot of care leavers end up trying to navigate family relationships, which can be tricky and complicated without support. Foster carers play a pivotal role way into the future, to think: 'Who will they spend Christmas with when they are 30, rather than now?' If children are leaving care without a variety of connections and relationships, then the system has not worked for them.*
> **(MIKE S, CARE-EXPERIENCED SOCIAL WORKER)**

So it's helpful that people, including you as our carer, and our social workers, can help us to build networks and rebuild any broken or fractured relationships that we wish to.

Invite us into your family

One of the ways that you can help us to feel that we belong as part of your family and home is to introduce us to your family members, and, if possible, invite us to be a part of your family unit. If you're introducing us to other members of your family, please talk to us first, so that we can think about how we want you to refer to us. Sometimes saying that we are your 'foster child' can make us feel different and disconnected from you. But we all might have different views on this, so it's best to ask, then we can work out what feels most comfortable for us and you.

It helps when we understand who people are, how they're related, and can think about what they might mean to us going forward. (Are they going to be someone who will be popping round to the house a lot, or are they someone we might see once a year, and are they going to want to see us as a part of their family too?) We can feel more part of the family by having an idea about family stories (and not just the happy ones), and any shared jokes or traditions, but not too many too quickly or this might feel overwhelming. Just weave it all in naturally.

Make links in the local community

Being involved in the wider community somehow can help you to feel as if you fit in and belong somewhere too. Kim was always involved in her church community, which became her church family and gave her key people to call on when things were going wrong. Knowing that support was always there from these key people was invaluable. When we have those community connections, we have a group of people who can support us, and we feel part of something bigger, which can continue once we leave care. This way we won't feel that we need to fully start afresh and won't feel fully alone. It creates a sense of stability, as the community becomes a constant when everything else might feel transitional and chaotic.

Sometimes when we move into a new foster home, we are moving to a completely new place. It can be hard to stay connected with previous friends and relationships, especially where there's distance involved, and we can end up feeling really isolated. Being a kid means that moving a few towns away can seem a real distance. When we have to move to a new area or a new school (such as one closer to our new foster home), we're starting again from scratch, knowing no one. We can feel as if we don't really know where we are or who's around us. We feel awkward and out of place. When we move a lot, we can end up searching for something, anything, that feels familiar or even just okay, but then we never quite find it before we move on again.

CJ moved during the Covid-19 pandemic too, which made him feel even more isolated as he went straight into lockdown in his new home, going months without really seeing anyone he knew. With it being the pandemic, he wasn't going into school either so wasn't seeing his friends as much as he usually would. Being in a completely new place with completely new people can leave you feeling lonely in your own home.

Friendships

When you feel disconnected from your area, and the people around you, your relationships in your foster home become even more essential. CJ's relationships with the other young people in his foster home were so important. He felt lucky there were other young people there to hang about with. Although after a while he realized these young people were quite different from him, these relationships were better than nothing. They connected, shared an experience, and offered some level of understanding and mutual respect to each other. They shared an understanding that they'd all been through situations and things that had led them to living in foster care and there was an unspoken agreement of what was okay and not okay to talk about.

Help us to keep long-term friendships going

> *Becoming and staying friends is usually due to care and authenticity, rather than necessity.* (CJ)

Longer-term relationships such as friendships are vital, as they're connections that have naturally occurred, rather than happening out of necessity (not knowing anyone and trying to form some connections). We'll have some shared experiences and hopefully positive memories with these friends. There are things within those relationships to look back on, and to continue to build on. It's likely that we'll feel safer and more willing to let our guard down in these longer-term relationships. There's more trust and feeling of authenticity – this person has chosen to remain our friend, and has made the effort to maintain this connection, despite the changes or distance.

With a new friendship, it's hard to know if that person is likely to stick around or not. It also might not be clear to us if *we* will be sticking around for long, especially if we've moved several times before. This means that it might not seem worth investing in new relationships. Where we have longer-term friendships that have formed authentically and naturally, then there can be a sense of loyalty as we've decided to come together and stay in touch. We've decided to stick together through difficult times.

When we can't see our people a lot, having opportunities to message or phone them (or talk online or play video games together) can be so important. Although it's not the same as going and seeing them in person, it can help as we're more able to talk to people we're familiar with, who we know, who know us, and who have some understanding of who we are – they hold a sense of our identity for us. This can give us a break from constantly talking to new people who know nothing about us, which can be a bit exhausting. New friendships can sometimes feel a bit forced and can stem from 'needing to do things' to 'meet new people'. So ideally, helping us to keep our longer-term friendships is usually worth doing. But we also recognize that sometimes we might need to meet new people who live closer to our new home too.

How to support us to find true friends

Making new friends can be tough and quite uncomfortable at times, especially as we get older. Sometimes it can be tempting to take us to events where we can meet other young people in care and hope we'll make new friends there. This can sometimes be helpful, as in CJ's example above. But it's important to remember that all young people in care are different, so just because they have the shared experience of being in care, it doesn't mean that they'll want to spend time together or get on.

> *One of the things that used to bother me is that I would always get invited to care-experienced events. Although I enjoyed these events, I wanted to meet people who were just young people, not just focused on care-experienced young people. I think adults in my life were expecting that I would find people like me at these events, but everyone was really different, and I never felt a sense of belonging.* (AMY)

It can be easier to make friends through doing activities you enjoy, meaning you naturally have similar interests. You could find activities or groups we can join that align with our interests where we can socialize. For CJ, this was going to the gym. When he started to go to the gym, he began to make more friends and had access to a much wider social circle, which led him to feel less isolated. Having the opportunity of shared experiences with others where memories can be built can 'fast track' the building of new friendships a little.

Summary

As we might have moved around a lot, or ended up with broken relationships, you can have a key role in supporting us to keep our relationships going with those we care about, helping us to think about mending difficult relationships, or navigating contact with those who we're less sure about seeing. Relationships, connections, and networks are important to anyone, but especially to us, as they help us to keep a sense of ourselves and our stories through time and have the potential to keep being our people when we eventually move out of care. In the next chapter, we think about when we've had relationships in the past that have been difficult or even abusive, how they might have affected our views of ourselves and how others might treat us, and how you can help us to understand and develop more positive relationships in the future.

CHAPTER 5

Understanding What Healthy Relationships Look Like

As we explored in Chapter 3, we all have our own individual story which led to us being in foster care. But often our stories include difficult, unhealthy, or even abusive relationships growing up. So we might understandably find it hard to trust or feel safe with other people. We also might not know what a healthy or good relationship really looks like, if we've not experienced one ourselves. In this chapter, we explore how difficult or unhealthy relationships can impact our views of relationships and how we might behave in them. Then we'll think about how you, as foster carers, can help us to learn what a healthy relationship looks like, so we can choose the relationships we want, and how we want to be in them, in the future.

Feeling 'different'

Being in care can have a really big impact on how we see ourselves, and our identity, and how other people see us too. We might feel shame, as if being in care is something we should avoid talking about or even hide from others. This can also affect how we might interact with others around us, as we might worry about them judging us, asking too many questions, or knowing too much about our lives.

> *In school, they would use 'you're in care' as an insult, not realizing that I actually was. I used to be so ashamed of being in foster care. But now I've met so many people who have been through what I've been through, and now I'm ashamed that I was so ashamed.* (ANGEL)

Sometimes this can lead us to feel like a bit of an outsider or see ourselves as different from other people. Amy describes often feeling like an imposter. Sometimes walking into a room, looking around, and thinking, 'No, I don't quite belong here.' It might be that in some situations we can be quite confident, but in others we might feel as if it's just too much. It can feel as if you can't have a 'normal' relationship, because all the relationships you've had in your life so far have been harmful or unsafe. It can sometimes make us feel uncomfortable socially and can lead us to keep people at a distance.

Losing trust

When we experienced difficult relationships in our early lives, or a lot of loss or rejection, this can change our views of relationships and what they should be like. For example, if we've been treated badly by those around us, we might start to believe that we should, and will, be treated the same in future relationships, and don't deserve anything better. It might be that people have responded to us in an unhelpful or even abusive way in the past, so we've learned to expect those same responses from our carers or friends. So we might react in a particular way to protect ourselves or defend against what we're expecting to happen. Early life experiences can also make it hard to trust people we meet, so we might end up not getting close to anyone. It can feel too difficult or scary to have a deep relationship.

> *I have friends, but all surface level friends. In the ways in which people would have that natural go-to instinct to go to people and rely on them in times of need, I don't have that. I find it hard to trust other people.* (ANGEL)

Getting close to people can be understandably hard, because

when children in care have been hurt or had unhealthy relationships in the past, they can find it hard to trust. They may even end up 'hurting others' or rejecting others first, to avoid being hurt themselves. But if their foster carers react to this by pulling away or acting angrily back, this can reinforce how the child might feel. 'Of course you're angry at me, and don't want to be around me any more. Everyone leaves me in the end.'

We might have learned that we shouldn't trust other people, as they tend to hurt us or let us down.

> *You struggle trusting people, don't really feel that you can put your faith in anyone any more, and that can lead you to feel quite lonely sometimes.* (MIA)

Even when it might seem that we want to be alone, or that we're good at being alone, this might have happened because we haven't had any other safe option. It would still be nice sometimes to have the choice of having someone there who we can rely on to help or support us.

How we might cope with relationships

It's often hard to know how to be in relationships, if we've not had many good ones so far, and especially if we're struggling to trust other people. We might end up keeping people at a bit of a distance if we don't trust them, which might feel safer, but means that we aren't really close to anyone. We might keep everything at a transactional or surface level, as this might feel a bit safer. We might worry about being hurt or people leaving if we were to let them in. Or we might rely on others for practical things but not rely on them emotionally.

> *Everything in relationships can sometimes feel quite transactional, which can make me feel quite sad.* (MIA)

We also may have a big worry that people will leave us. We might start to think that people who get to know us properly are going to get sick of us at some point and go somewhere else. This can often stem from a belief that, 'If my parents didn't want me that badly, then why would anyone else?' Even when things seem to be going well in a relationship, this can feel even scarier, as we *know* that they're going to leave us at some point, which will really hurt. So we might end up trying to be the 'perfect' foster child at first, following all the rules and hoping that you'll accept us, but this is hard to keep up.

> *You mask a lot in foster care. Try to be as perfect as possible on the basis that if I'm good, it might work out. Six months into it, I would still keep up appearances as much as possible.* (AMY)

Sometimes we might be living with foster carers for a while, and feel a bit more settled, so we might be okay enough to let all the trauma and distress out, to show some of the hurt we've gone through, and some of the ways that we really feel. But in our experience, this can lead to carers sometimes starting to panic and thinking, 'Oh, I can't do this.'

They might not know what's going on and think that we're being 'challenging'. But it actually might mean that we're feeling a bit safer with them than we were before, so our trauma is starting to come out. In that scenario, it's even more difficult when our carers give up on us, as it makes it even harder for us to trust anyone. It feels as if no one can handle us if we let them in or show them how we're really feeling.

It can sometimes be that 'hurt people end up hurting people' – this can sound quite cliché, but it can be true. When someone doesn't realize that they've been hurt, or how being hurt in the past has affected their relationships, then it can lead them to unintentionally hurt other people too. They might act on their emotions, feeling that they need to hurt the other person because they feel hurt themselves. This can be hard, as it might be a pattern that they're used to in relationships, so it's a pattern that they expect to happen again.

Managing conflict

If we've not been exposed to healthy relationships before, we might just not know how to manage conflict. We might end up repeating ways of being in relationships that we've seen before but that are unhealthy or even toxic. Or we might want to do things differently. Instead, we might have found our own ways to end an argument, but we might struggle to make things feel okay again. Or we might end up appeasing the other person to end the conflict (and putting up with too much), rather than sharing our own view. Or we might end up feeling angry and being aggressive to try to dominate or control the other person to help us to feel safer ourselves. It might be that what we do in relationships when we're feeling unsafe, or are trying to manage conflict in our own way, ends up being detrimental to the relationships that we're in, which can lead to the breakdown or ending of relationships, and lead to us feeling alone or lonely again.

CJ talks about how now he has had experience of being in romantic relationships, and has matured a lot, he sees things differently and can more easily see the bigger picture. In previous relationships he would get into arguments instead of talking, and would close off instead of sharing. But now he prioritizes good communication and opening up about things.

Sadly, a high proportion of care leavers are in abusive relationships where there's domestic violence. They might be seeking love from wherever they can seemingly get it, and they might not fully know what love is. They might just want to be loved (as anyone does) and may go to any means to get it. So they might end up in vulnerable situations where others can take advantage of them, as they don't know that they deserve much more. They might not know that the love they are seeking is not healthy, because if they've come from a broken home, and all they've seen is abuse and violence, then it can feel normal to them. It has been their everyday reality. And if they don't know that they deserve any better, they can end up settling in these abusive relationships, as perhaps that's the way that they've always been treated.

If we haven't had experience of positive relationships growing up, and if we haven't had positive relationship skills modelled to us (e.g. how to manage conflict, or how to repair a relationship – what to do when things go wrong), then we're unlikely to know what to do when this happens. People aren't born with these skills; they learn them through being around other people and through being in relationships. When we've had bad experiences of relationships in the past, this can mean that our new relationships might be short lived, we might end up in abusive relationships, or might struggle to get into relationships at all.

How you can help

As we described above, often when young people have been taken away from their birth family for various reasons, and have been living in care, it's likely that they have experienced unhealthy, or even abusive, relationships. These relationships can become a template for how they understand what future relationships should and will look like for them, what to expect from the other person, and how they're likely to be treated. It is therefore really important to think about how you can support the young people in your care to understand what 'healthy' relationships look like and to know that they deserve them.

Young people might have witnessed relationships close to them (such as their own parents' relationship, or how their parents interacted with them) which have been unhealthy or abusive. For example, they might have seen lots of shouting and conflict, and trying to hurt each other emotionally and physically, and might have started to view this as the way that relationships really are. That's all they know. When they're able to witness or experience something different, such as couples being (appropriately) affectionate with one another, taking the time to be with each other, and supporting each other through challenges, then this starts to show what good, healthy relationships can look like. So one of the most important ways of helping us to understand what healthy relationships look like is to allow us to experience them ourselves. This can include building a healthy relationship with us, little by little, and allowing us to see healthy relationship dynamics within your home (such as between foster carers (if you're in a couple), and with your other family members). Modelling healthy relationship skills within your own relationships is paramount.

Relationships with you as foster carers can be a way to help us to have an experience of a healthy relationship, and learn what this looks and feels like. This is one of the biggest responsibilities for foster carers: creating safe, trusting relationships with the child, and the child having someone whom they can talk to and confide in, and make mistakes with, knowing that the relationship will be repaired when they do. It's also important to find ways to let us know that you're planning to stick around, be there for us, and help us.

It might sound really simple, but it's all about just being there.

That's what it really comes down to. When you have someone who's there, and who's willing to listen and support you whatever happens, and offer guidance, that means a lot. Even if we're struggling to trust that you'll stick around, being there and being consistent over time can help us to start to trust in this. It's about reassuring us that you're planning to be there, and you don't plan on going anywhere else.

When supporting us, it's important to recognize that we'll likely not have had the same experience of relationships as you have. If you have a home with lots of healthy relationships, this is great, but also might take a bit of getting used to for us. If we've been through numerous difficult relationships in our lives, and then we arrive somewhere where relationships are done in a completely different way from what we're used to, that can feel very scary. We might feel quite hesitant and overwhelmed, and could try to retreat. It might take a while for us to understand that these new ways of being in relationships are okay and safe, so it's important to pace this, rather than 'forcing' it on us straight away. It can be useful to introduce new ways of doing things in segments (e.g. this is how we communicate here, and how we talk together when things go wrong).

When disagreements, difficult conversations, or even everyday interactions remain calm, this might feel like a dangerous situation to us because it might be so unfamiliar. We might be thinking that things are so peaceful we need to stay alert and on edge, as something is surely going to go wrong. Or we may think that you're trying to trip us up. This can sometimes lead us to 'self-sabotage' or react in a way that we would have in our previous home, as this could feel safer. We might expect you to react by shouting or becoming angry, because this will feel more familiar to us. But if you can remain calm, and notice and talk to us about it and how we might be feeling, then this can help us to adapt to this new way of being in relationships, over time. Please be patient with us.

Help us with other relationships

One of the ways that we learn how to have healthy relationships is to try them out, make mistakes, and find out what works. You can also help us with this, by being there for us to talk to, and sometimes give advice (although we might not always want to hear it).

CJ describes how the first thing that really helped him to reflect on his relationships and what a healthy relationship should look like was a poem that was shared with him when he was in care. It had helped that the carer had not been too directive but had given him space to think and something to help him to reflect on what he'd been through, and what he might want going forward. Below, CJ describes eloquently the important messages that he's learned about what makes a relationship healthy or not, and some 'red flags'.

Unhealthy relationships are more parasitic, whereas healthy relationships are more symbiotic. If the relationship is healthier, you are building off each other, and supporting and enabling each other. Whereas if it is unhealthy, you are more likely to be taking things away from the other person to nourish yourself or vice versa. In unhealthy relationships, there is a big lack of trust in each other, and there is not an expectation that the other person will hold up to what they have said that they will do. The communication can be either non-existent, or harmful and damaging, trying to hurt the other person. How emotions are shown, and attended to, is also key. In an unhealthy relationship, the emotions are focused on, and often exacerbated by the other person – there is a focus on the symptom (the emotion) rather than the underlying issue. This expression of emotions without listening to or attempting to understand the other person can lead to the unhealthy dynamics escalating to boiling point. Where people remain curious and attuned to each other and try to explore the underlying cause of the emotion and address it, and meet each other on a similar emotional level (rather than trying to prove that they are feeling worse), this creates healthier relationship dynamics.

Healthy boundaries in relationships are also incredibly important. In an unhealthy relationship, the boundaries can either be so tall that they create such a big wall between the individuals that they cannot connect, or they are completely broken down to the extent that they are not considered, and the relationship can become intrusive and overbearing. (CJ)

When we struggle to find the words

Sometimes, even when we've started to trust you, it might still be hard to tell you when we're struggling or need your support. So it can help when you check in with us, and let us know that how we feel is okay (you're not scared by it), and that you want to be there and help us. It might be that we've not had this before, and adults around us might not have wanted to know how we were feeling, or might have ignored us or shouted at us when we were upset or worried. So this might feel quite new or scary.

Amy J used to struggle to communicate when she was feeling low, so she used a 'communication book': 'I would write how I was feeling, slide it under the door, and then they would come up and talk to me about it.' Diego had other ways of communicating with his carers.

I used to write songs about being in care and how I felt, and I would sing and my carer would listen and respond to that. You could tell she was listening to how I was feeling. I also played with my Barbie, even though I was 16. I used to role play a lot with dolls, like things I'd been through in my life. I'd play them out and that would start a conversation with my carer. (DIEGO)

One of the worst things that it can be easy to accidentally do is make the child feel that you don't get it. If we tell you something about how we feel, or about something that happened to us, or something we're worried about, and you say something like, 'It's not that bad, don't worry', you might be trying to reassure us or help us to think in a more positive way. But it can unintentionally make us feel worse, as we might feel that you don't understand us at all.

Or if we're talking to you about something we feel is important (especially if we don't usually open up), even if it doesn't sound particularly important to you, please try to take the time to listen, even if you're really busy. Sometimes it can take a lot of courage for us to decide to share something, and by missing this opportunity to be heard, we might feel ignored and dismissed, and may not feel safe to share things with you again. You might not know that it's an important conversation, but it is to us.

Understanding how and when to best communicate with us as an individual, unique child is a big part of building a trusting, strong relationship with us. You'll probably get this wrong at times, and that's fine, but listen to what we tell you and be ready to be vulnerable with us, and curious in a gentle way.

Joking and sarcasm

The kind of jokes that we make are important to be aware of, as sometimes they might be communicating something else, and can be a way of testing out how you'd respond. We can make jokes every single day, as a smile and laugh can be far easier than bursting out into tears. If we can turn something horrible that causes harm or distress into laughter, this can feel less difficult or weighty. It's therefore crucial to keep an eye on what we might be trying to communicate to you. For example, we might say something like, 'What good is an ashtray when you have my own skin to put out a cigarette on?' It can be a way of letting you know something serious (i.e. that talking about ashtrays brings back bad memories), in a lighter and easier way. It might also be a way of testing out how you would react to this – do you agree with it? Are you safe? It's important to see it as us trying to make a joke, trying to keep it light, but it's also important to let us know that what happened to us is not okay, even though we might be making a joke about it, and that you wouldn't do this to us, and that people care about us.

Make things okay again

Repairing relationships after conflict is crucial, because if we and you are left with uncomfortable feelings after a fallout, this can make things feel so much worse. If we've had an argument, it's likely we might feel that you've given up on us, that you won't be around for us any more, and that you'll leave us too. These feelings might make us put our barriers up even more, making it even less likely for us to trust you or feel safe with you going forward. You might experience our barriers going up badly too – you might feel rejected by us, upset, or even more angry at us.

So, the quicker we can make things feel okay between us again, the better. It can be through talking things through, although this might feel a bit too much at first, and we might need a bit more space. Or it could be just doing something to show that you still care. It might take time for things to feel okay, but please stick with us through it.

Summary

If we've had difficult or even abusive relationships growing up, which a lot of us have had, then it's difficult to know what a 'healthy' relationship looks like. We will have learned how to 'be' in relationships from those around us, so sometimes it can feel weird or awkward when we come into your home and things are done so differently. It's easy for us to fall back into old patterns of doing things, especially if we don't feel that we can trust you yet. One of the best ways for you to help us with our relationships is to show us (gently and over time) what good relationships look and feel like, and help us to know that we're worthy of them. As our relationship with you deepens, we can feel more trusting towards you, and we can lean on you when needed, then you'll be able to help us to get through more difficult times too, as we explore in the next chapter.

CHAPTER 6

Getting Through Difficult Days

Everyone has difficult days, whether you're a young person in care, a young person living with their family, or an adult (or foster carer). It's how we act on difficult days, and how that's understood and responded to by those around us, and supporting us, that's important. In this chapter, we think about which days and times might be particularly difficult for young people in care, how it's often not just the day, but the time surrounding it too which can be tough, and how to support us through these difficult times.

What do we mean by difficult days?

Difficult days can take lots of shapes and forms. Everyone's unique, and has their own individual experiences, which will influence which days might be particularly difficult for them. For young people in care, some of the shared main days that it's important to consider are:

- Mother's and Father's Day
- Christmas
- birthdays
- birthdays of parents
- birthdays of siblings or other important family members (especially when we are unable to see them)
- anniversaries of particular events (e.g. when we left our family home)
- anniversaries of bereavements.

It's important for you to remember when these dates happen and recognize that some of these might impact on us on a yearly basis. Sometimes foster carers and professionals might think that we shouldn't be upset about missing our family, as we were taken out of our family home for a reason. They might even think that we shouldn't miss our family as our parents were 'bad people'. No matter how bad or unhealthy our relationship with our parents or family might be, those family members may still really matter to us. It might take us some time to recognize what has happened in our early life, and to process and determine how we feel about it. But no matter what, there might still be some care there, and it's important for those around us to remain considerate of that.

Difficult days can include birthdays, Mother's Day and Father's Day, Christmas, any key anniversary like when they were brought into care, or when a loved one passed away. These days are not always obvious, and it may be that only the young person is aware of them; no one else might know. (DIEGO)

When we're not with our family on these significant days, it can feel difficult or weird. When we're in a home where there are new traditions and ways of doing things (especially during celebration times), this can make us feel isolated, alone, or different.

Poem by Amy J

'Twas the night before Christmas, when all through the town
Laughter was shared, despite the hidden frown
Upon a young girl's face who dreaded this time of year
For it brought up so much loss, rejection and fear
She, like so many, would lie awake in her bed
Wishing she could be happy instead of filled with dread
At the thought of waking on Christmas day
Knowing no one would be there to say
'Merry Christmas'

What you might notice on difficult days

Often, as a carer, you might see our reaction, or the 'outcome' of a difficult day, rather than seeing everything that happens. You send us to school, we come home, and then you get a report from school about all the problematic things that have happened during the day. You might be wondering what's gone on, as we seemed okay in the morning. It can then be helpful for you to explore with us what has been happening for us today, and how we've been feeling underneath what happened.

Or you might notice that we just don't seem ourselves. CJ has noticed that when lots of young people in care are having a difficult day, they might not want to get out of bed in the morning. We all know that realistically you have to get out of bed, especially as you get older. But everyone wakes up some mornings and thinks that they can't be bothered, that the day feels too much to face. When this happens, rather than arguing with us about it, it's important to remind us that we've all felt that way at times. It might be that we need a bit more time that morning to get up, or occasionally, actually, we might need the day off. We need to look after our emotional wellbeing too. Because although it's not the best thing to let your child stay off school, if it's on a day that they're really finding tough emotionally, it's a way to show us that you recognize that we're really struggling today and need some care and support. We acknowledge, however, that school attendance is important (see our chapter on education), so this should only be if your child really needs a day off due to their emotional distress. It should not be a regular thing.

The ABER model

When talking about how the time around difficult days can be experienced by young people within care, CJ came up with the

ABER model which we have included below. This shows the likely process of initial anticipation, a physical 'build up', the event, and then a subsequent release. This can be helpful in understanding that difficult days often affect not only the day, but also the time around it, and can impact young people in a number of ways. Where we can acknowledge and understand this, listen to what the young person needs at each stage, and be supportive, this can help to make difficult days more manageable.

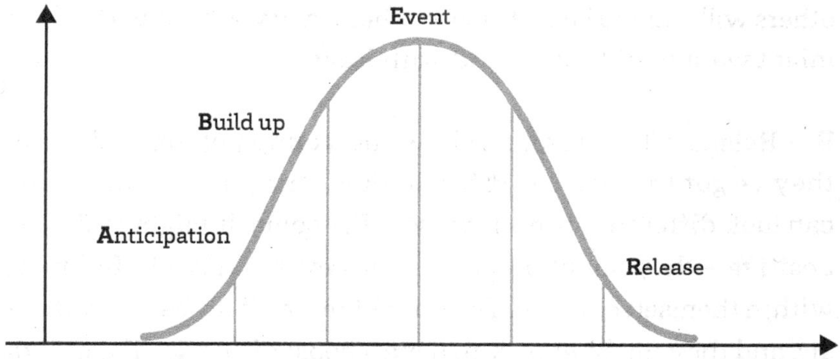

CJ's ABER model

A – Anticipation: This is the psychological build up to the day. The young person might start to overthink, start a countdown to the day in their head, with lots of anticipatory anxiety. They might start to ruminate about the day or what's happened in the past, and everything that came along with it. We might see this anticipatory anxiety and stress in how the young person copes – they withdraw (socially or emotionally) and become more isolated, or we might notice an impact on their eating (not eating enough/too little) or sleep.

B – Build up: This refers to the physical build up that the young person might experience due to the emotional stress of it all. They might seem physically tense or on edge and jumpy. They might appear fatigued or experience physical reactions such as headaches or migraines. They might struggle with emotional regulation (lots of emotional outbursts) or might seem quite irritable.

E – Event: This is *the* difficult day. Different days will be difficult for different young people, and this will depend on their unique experiences and what's important to them. Sometimes young people will prefer to just get on with their usual everyday things, others will want to be distracted, others may want support, others might want to hide away and withdraw.

R – Release: This refers to how the young person feels after they've got through the difficult day. This post-event release can look different for each person. For some, it might feel more positive – they might be glad that it's over and might feel more within themselves again. They might feel as if it's been a catharsis, and they might appear to have a boost of energy. For others, they might feel the physical effects of having experienced lots of anxiety and stress. They might feel drained, fatigued, might want to sleep or rest for longer than usual or stay in bed; they might try to bury themselves in work or hobbies, or they might seem low in mood. They might take a bit of time to feel okay again.

How to talk to us about difficult days

As mentioned earlier, it's really important that, as a carer, you recognize that there can be a process of getting through difficult days, and that we might struggle during the period around it, not just on the day.

Your approach towards these days needs to be empathic and understanding. It can help to wonder about what it is within the day that has caused us to feel the way that we do. Sometimes when you ask us directly why we've behaved in a particular way, you might not get anywhere. This can be a difficult question for anyone to answer! But if you're curious and gentle with your questioning, this can help. It can start with the understanding that we might have something on our mind, noticing this, and being curious about it: 'I've noticed that you don't seem yourself today; what's up?' Or, 'You look as if something is on your mind. Do you want to talk about it? Is it anything that I can help with?'

The best way you can approach this with us can be to give us space, allow us to take the lead and let you know what we need, and support us to come to you if we wish to. It's not often helpful to say, for example, 'It's Mother's/Father's Day; do you want to talk about what is in your head?' Instead, you might say, 'I'm aware that today might be a really difficult day for you. You don't have to talk about it, but if you would like to, I'm here.' It's important to try to create a safe space for us to freely express how we feel, so that we know that whatever we say to you is acceptable for you, that you will accept it, and can handle it.

It might be that you worry about not being able to empathize because you haven't been through the same situation as us before, so you won't be able to fully understand what we're experiencing. This shouldn't get in the way of you helping us to feel safe and understood. CJ spoke about feeling isolated as a foster child. He knew that his experiences were not unique as such, but they also were not too common. So initially he tried to find people who related to his exact experiences. He tried to find acceptance and understanding within other people. But he later realized that it's possible for people to build that understanding even if they've not had the exact same experience, as they might have experienced a similar feeling instead.

So it can be useful for you to empathize with the emotions, fears, anger, or upset that we have, even if you cannot truly understand what the experience was like. What exactly the day is, isn't always the most important thing – it's how we're feeling about it, making sense of it, and reacting to it.

Support us to cope with difficult days

People cope with difficult days in different ways. Some people like to shut themselves off on their difficult days, preferring to be alone, soaking it all in, and experiencing their feelings. But some people don't like to do that and want to throw themselves into other things like their work, a hobby, or a substance. We manage our difficult days in different ways, and there shouldn't be an expectation for another person to manage theirs in the same way. So just because you find a particular strategy helpful, it doesn't mean that your foster child will find it helpful too. It's important to allow and help us to find ways which work for us as an individual. If you find that some of our ways of coping seem to be quite unhealthy, it's good to try to encourage more healthy ways to manage things – but ways that work for us.

Even as an adult now, when the days roll around that are annually very difficult for me, I like to have what I call a 'rot day', which means I basically sit in bed all day in my fluffy pyjamas, watching TV, while I drink lots of cups of tea and order takeaways. My partner knows me enough to understand this and will basically spend the day doing this with me. Although I recognize that this may not be what people consider a healthy approach to a bad day, one day like this makes things feel manageable for me and then I'm fine the next day. When I was a child in foster care, it would have been really helpful if my foster carers had been able to understand this, but I think there's a lot of emphasis on 'healthy approaches' so it was probably difficult to see this as a solution. In my view, the most important thing is to be open, creative, and led by your foster child in these situations. (MIA)

It's also important to approach us on our own terms and think with us about what support we might want from you. What this looks like can really differ, in terms of what helps us individually, but also what type of difficult day it is.

When a difficult day brings up memories

If it's a difficult day that brings up lots of memories, we might want to have space to talk through them with someone. We might want to talk about what's important to us about the day, share memories, visit somewhere, or look through photos. Or if it's difficult memories, or times when we remember something that we don't want to, we might want space to talk about what we've remembered in a safe way, or we might want to be distracted by doing another activity with you, or 'escape' to somewhere else for the day. Sometimes it's helpful to completely ignore the memory, but sometimes it's better not to. What we need may change too, so it can be helpful to check out with us what we need in that moment to feel okay, or to be able to cope with what we're experiencing.

When you open your house to a kid like me from a challenging life and a different culture, you need to understand even just a little bit of what that kid is going through. Everyone is different and will want to cope differently. All different ways of giving support can be fine, but it can help for the foster family to be able to see the perspective of the kid. For example, for me, when I've gone through shit, I don't want to explain it to someone, and I want other people to know that I don't want to explain it. Just make sure I'm breathing and acknowledge me, but know I don't wanna talk. It's more about you showing you're acknowledging what they are going through, showing them you care, but leaving them alone. (NOOR)

Talk through the 'what-if' worries

If we're full of anxiety or fear, sometimes talking these fears through with someone can be helpful. CJ says that when he is feeling anxious about something, he finds it helpful when someone talks through the 'what-if' worries he has about a scenario, to help him to disprove them. He finds that this can help him to de-escalate something that felt like a big worry to something that doesn't feel like a possibility any more.

We know that anxious thinking can lead to more anxious thinking, so it's important that if we share a worry (or 'what if') with you, that you don't accidentally add more, which can amplify our anxiety. Instead, try to help us think about evidence against the 'what if'; reasons why the 'what-if' scenario wouldn't work. This can then help us to feel hopeful that our worries will not become real-life scenarios. It's also important not to dismiss our worries and just say that they are untrue, without exploring them. Our worries will have some truth and reasonable concern underneath them, and so our anxieties and fears are understandable. Helping us to understand this, but also be able to challenge them with you, can help us to feel okay again.

It's helpful for us to know that every difficult day will eventually pass. However, this isn't always the best thing to say in the moment. We all know that it's realistically going to pass, but it doesn't feel like that when we're experiencing it, so there's a danger that it can sound dismissive, and it might lead us to close up and not want to talk about it any more.

Please also try to gently break down any possible walls that we might have put up, so that we know there's help there, and we're not alone in dealing with it – even if we're not ready to talk about it quite yet.

Summary

We'll all have difficult days, but for young people in foster care, there are some that might remind them of the past, difficult memories, or people they're missing. There might be periods of time around these difficult days where you might notice that we are impacted by them, or you might even end up seeing the 'outcome' of the difficult day rather than how it has affected us initially. Try to be curious and empathetic about this where you can. Let us take the lead – let us know that you're there to support us and that you're happy to talk things through if and when we want to. Ask us what support we might need from you, and know that this might change over time, and suddenly. The support that you offer us can really help, but also, we might need to sometimes access other services too. In Chapter 7, we think about how you can support us with the other services, professionals, and meetings that we might need to attend.

CHAPTER 7

Supporting Us with Professional Networks

Often, as a young person in care, we'll have lots of different professionals and services supporting us, such as social workers or mental health services. This can be a real challenge, as it's lots of different relationships for us to navigate, lots of appointments, and usually lots of different people coming in and out of our lives. In this chapter, we think about what it's like for us with all these professionals and services involved, and how support from you can help. We'll talk about how you, as a foster carer, can make us feel more comfortable in these meetings, support us to make choices and feel safe to express our views and opinions and represent ourselves, and what your role might be.

The importance of a professional support network

Having a good network of services around us can help us to feel that we matter. For some of us, coming from backgrounds where we might have had no one, when we've had to rely on ourselves, it can feel a bit strange at first, and it might take a bit of time to get used to.

> *You feel like you are human, like you are important, you are something. When you have had nothing for all of that time, it can feel a shock. You feel alive, you feel human because someone cares. It's refreshing – ah, someone cares!* (NOOR)

When we're talking about a professional support network, we're really thinking about people who can help us to get through tough times and be there when we need them.

It's so important to have the chance to build a trusting relationship with a professional, where we can talk about any worries we have, and check things out. This isn't just someone to whom we can come when things are going wrong, but someone we can build that relationship with, who is alongside us. Because when we have that trust, we're more likely to speak to that person when we need to, someone who is there with us throughout our journeys. We're not going to open up about our business to a random stranger. We're more likely to talk to someone we trust, someone who knows us, someone who understands us.

Kim recalls a number of people who've been particularly important to her and part of her support network. There was a pastoral lead who supported her through high school, and beyond, and a mentor from the Children's Society. She viewed these as her outlets, and people she could approach to talk about everyday things that were on her mind, such as if she had had an argument with someone. They were key people who could help her get through tough times.

Changes in professionals

Pretty much any young person in care will have had lots of changes in the professionals supporting them. It would be so much better if we could have the same people all along, but that rarely happens. Sometimes we have so many changes that we don't even know who our professionals are. It can make us feel as if we are 'just a number' and don't matter. Kim talks about being at university and not hearing from her social worker. Then when she got in touch with social care, she was told that her social worker had left and that she must have 'fallen through the cracks' of the system as no one had been allocated to her. Kim was aware that she often seemed very independent and capable, but despite this, she still needed some help and support, as everyone does.

It can be hard to trust in new professionals too. We might have had bad experiences with professionals before and given up on building relationships because we *knew* that they were going to leave too so it wasn't worth bothering with them, or we might feel let down by them. We might think, 'You guys suck. Why should I trust you?' So, the professional needs to prove themselves and earn that trust.

Amy talks about how she had a personal advisor (PA) with whom she built up a relationship over nine years. She really invested in this relationship, and it had started to feel like a friendship as they'd known each other for so long and had been through many difficult times together. Then, when Amy turned 25, she suddenly no longer had a PA. Although her PA sent her a nice card, this was still really difficult. The PA had been someone stable for Amy, someone she'd been able to go to for support for nine years, and suddenly this option was removed. It felt like a harsh reality, and another attachment that was severed.

So please bear with us if it takes us some time to be okay with the professionals and services we work with. Try to understand why this might be tough.

Our experiences of social care meetings

As children in care, we're expected to go to lots of meetings about us, which is a bit weird. If we don't go, they happen anyway without us, but still about us, which can be even stranger.

Attending our social care meetings (like looked after children reviews) in a room with lots of adults, many of whom we don't know, or even joining online, can feel like an exposing experience. We get asked lots of basic questions about our lives, but strange ones too, and ones that feel really intrusive. As Mia says, it can feel quite robotic, too formal, and like a tick-box exercise. She used to describe herself as feeling like a barcode number to her social worker, one of who knows how many. There were questions such as, 'How is your health?' 'How is your education?' As a young person, you don't understand why these are the only things being asked.

A tick-box process or true support

> *It's just like a tick-box process. They don't get to know you. It doesn't feel meaningful to you and it just makes work for them. I don't really see the point in it. Just scrap that Health and Care Plan. They are all the same, every year. They would ask you what you are interested in, and I would be, like nothing, or maybe I would play guitar or something. But then they would put down, 'Ooh, she needs guitar lessons.' Or if I said I enjoyed playing tennis once, it'd be like, 'Oh God, they're gonna force me to play tennis again.' So I just wouldn't say anything. Not everyone has or needs a hobby. But they make you think you're weird if you just want to come home, watch TV, and see your friends. Isn't that what most kids do? I felt they forced things on me to feel like a normal child, but by doing that, they made me feel abnormal, because it's not natural.* (ANGEL)

It can also feel as if the person who asks doesn't really want to know the answer, but they've been told they *have to* ask the question, because it's part of the process, not because they really care or are interested. They might seem to be listening, and write down what we say, but then they don't actually act on it.

Other questions can feel way too personal to talk about, or even worse, be talked about by other people.

> *I used to find them [social care meetings] funny, as they would ask me the same thing every month. I'm not going to answer that, because that's another part of my life that you are going to get all involved in. It makes you hide things. It becomes a bit of a game, or it did to me. You can tell the difference between someone coming out and asking if you're okay, rather than 'I have to get this tick box done.' In my meetings, I used to enjoy going to them, but I felt like I was in a TV show sometimes.* (MIA)

It can also not feel okay when you keep being asked the same embarrassing question, such as whether you are 'sexually active'. Just because we might have a new boyfriend or girlfriend, or partner, it doesn't mean that it's okay to keep asking us about safe sex and then talking about it in a meeting. It sometimes feels that because we've said a particular 'buzz word', everyone's going to suddenly rush in to 'implement' this, this, and that.

Embarrassment about talking about feelings with professionals we don't know well

It's hard having your life talked about by other people. In the meetings, they might ask, 'How are you doing?' But you might have had a month where everything has been chaotic, and your social workers are at their wits' end. So what do you answer then? Do you say everything's fine and sugarcoat it? Or should you be honest, but then have to talk in detail about everything that's gone wrong? It can feel a bit ridiculous at times. No other 16-year-old, who isn't in care, is having to sit in a meeting with their school headteacher, the health nurse who they've probably only met once (if that), and their social worker, and talk about really personal things such as if they are sexually active or why they were home late the other night. Please think about what you talk about in these meetings, as it can feel embarrassing and too much. It can also feel as if we're being treated and judged differently from other children. Some kids would be grounded for smoking, and others wouldn't, whereas if we do anything like that, sometimes it can seem as if it's the worst thing in the world.

If there are problems or challenges at home, it's best to try and sort out any issues before the meeting, rather than getting everyone involved. If we can get things sorted first, then do we really have to bring them up in the meeting again, with everyone there? As Mia says, 'It's like your mum calling the GP or school every time she doesn't like what you're doing.' When a problem is talked about, and everyone jumps in, it can feel as if everyone is against you, so it's easy to deny things or end up lying about everything.

> *I felt like although professionals want you to tell the truth, sometimes it can be like they want you to tell them what they want you to say, rather than what you really want to say.* (MIA)

One of the good things about the meetings is that they give us space to speak up and say if we're unhappy about anything. That is, if we're confident doing so. Also, we're getting to actually hear the information, so we know what people are saying about us. But that's only if we go along. If not, there are lots of people talking about us, and making judgements about us, when we're not even there. It can make us stress about what they're talking about.

Going along to a meeting about you can be scary, and you can get a bit nervous before it. You have all these people coming in to what's supposed to be your home. They give you the choice if you want to come, but it would be better if it wasn't even called a meeting, and if we were given choices about what it looks like. Perhaps they could make it informal, giving us different ways of sharing the information, or going out for a cup of tea or some food to talk.

Health check-ups are another strange one. You would never have to do these if you weren't in care, so why do we have to do them? It feels as if we've been observed and our health has been documented in detail ever since we went into care, and for some of us, ever since we were born. Again, this can feel like a tick-box exercise.

> *They might ask, 'Are you okay?' but they don't create a safe environment for you to actually say how you are, so it's easier to just say, 'I'm fine'. They just go through a blanket form of things to check off without thinking of the impact of those things – are those things important? I used to think I was being paranoid, thinking they thought I was fat when they weighed me. But then I got access to my records and that's pretty much all they said about me, that I needed to lose weight.* **(ANGEL)**

Experiences of mental health services

When people come out and ask you questions, you know that they have an agenda. For example, with mental health support, you feel as though you have to say yes to things. You feel compelled to do things. But this means that support isn't meaningful if we don't really want to do it, or if we aren't asking for that type of support. We might just be saying yes because we think that it's the 'right' thing to do. So it's important to check how we really feel and give us proper choices, without pressure to do what other people expect us to do.

> *I didn't have a good experience of child and adolescent mental health services (CAMHS). The social worker came round, and I just agreed to go. But then I withdrew and refused to go, and people were really upset and annoyed with me. I was given a choice, but it wasn't really a choice.* **(MIA)**

Some young people will find mental health services really useful to help with emotions, or to better understand the past.

> *You don't know the words to use as a child, because you don't understand what you've been through. And that's why you need things like CAMHS to give you the words to describe it.* **(ANGEL)**

But it's also so hard when you get the help that you need from somewhere, and you've decided to trust people and let them in, and they are so lovely and supportive, but then they tell you that you're getting too old for children's mental health services, or you have to stop going.

Sometimes we might not know that we need to access support, so it can help if you've had the training needed to spot the signs that we might be struggling with our mental health, then you can help us to get relevant support.

Some carers might think that any child who is a little bit naughty has got attention deficit hyperactivity disorder (ADHD), but they might just like to express themselves. What's most important is that they are able to have a sit-down conversation with the child first, asking them about what's going on, and then seek further support and advice. (SHANNON)

When professionals meet with us, they sometimes share notes with our carers. Often, we might like it better when people show us the notes that they write, or if they're going to take notes, they ask if it's okay. Professionals should be respectful about the information we give to them, and talk to us about who they plan to share that information with and why.

How to help us to make decisions

Most young people have their parents, or other adults around them, to help them to make big decisions about their lives (and make sure that they don't make bad ones, or if they do, that they've thought it through first). So for us, it's you as our carers.

It's essential that when you're helping us with decisions, you don't put your own agenda on us, and know that our decisions are our decisions. Even if you don't realize it, it's likely that you'll have your own agenda about what you think is best for us. It's just about being open minded to things.

When I was younger, I went to college five separate times, as each time I went something happened. I couldn't cope

> *with the pressure of the first course, and I tend to be quite a perfectionist. Rather than asking me what I wanted to do, and what I thought could be a good next option for me, it felt like my carers focused more on what I hadn't done. I don't think anyone ever asked me what I actually wanted to do next.* **(REBECCA)**

It can be that we worry about choosing an option that we want, as other people might see it as 'wrong' or it might upset them. For example, if we want to spend time with our family, and we're asked about this, we might worry that we'll offend you or upset you. We might feel really torn loyalties with this one. We know that you, as our carer, are trying to do lots of good things for us, as everyone always tells us, so we feel that we should be grateful and not do anything 'wrong'. So if you can reassure us that you'll be okay, and be here for us whatever we decide in the end, that can be really reassuring.

Sometimes it can also feel as if we aren't asked about what we want to happen and that decisions are made for us and we have to go along with them or we will be seen as 'disengaged' or ungrateful for the support. But often we know that it wouldn't work for us, and maybe we want something else instead. We often know best what's going to be helpful for us, or not.

> *When you're in a family unit and something is going on, you have a discussion about what you want to do, and what you think you need. In my experience, there was not a discussion about that. I remember being in my bed, when I wouldn't get up, eat, or drink. My foster carer was on the phone to the social worker, not knowing what to do. The*

> *social worker wanted me to see CAMHS. I agreed to the first appointment, but by the next one I said that I wasn't going again. So I really had to fight them about what I wanted. I said that I'd been looking online about this, and researched about what might help.* (REBECCA)

Some of us might be quite confident and well spoken, but lots of us aren't, so we might feel that we can't speak up. We might end up going along with what we think that the adults want us to do. We get that the foster carer and other professionals just want to do what they think is the right thing, but they can get so wrapped up in what they see as right that they don't always see what *we* want to do. So please be a bit more open to what we're saying and give us some trust. It might be that we try out something that we want to do and it goes wrong, but isn't that part of life? Professionals try things out to support young people all the time, so if they can have a trial, why can't it work that way for us too?

As we get older, it's also important to allow us to make bad decisions at times, as long as we stay safe. As long as we have capacity, we're allowed to make bad choices, even if they don't suit what adults around us think that we should do. Every 16-year-old is going to make bad decisions at some point. That's just part of growing up.

> *The ideal foster carer would be trustful of the person they are caring for, and would advise but allow autonomy, and roll with it.* (AMY)

Speaking up and advocacy

Sometimes we might feel that we have something we really want to say, and we feel confident enough to speak up and share our view, or even challenge what's being said. But sometimes we might need some help with this too. As our carer, you might help us to practise this, or think about what we want to say and how. Your role might then be taking a bit of a backseat in those meetings, but being around to help us if we need it, and offering your own feedback when asked. You can help us to come up with solutions for any challenges that are being talked about, while holding our own needs, wants, and goals in mind. But if we don't want to attend, or speak up, don't force us.

Sometimes, it might help if you can raise some things on our behalf, if we don't feel confident enough to. To do this, it might be that you talk to us before a meeting, think about what we want to say, and how we want to say it. You might then help to make space for us to share our views, or encourage us gently to speak up, offering us reassurance and support at the time. Or it might be that we're happier for you to say it for us – but if you do, please check with us that you're getting it right, and that you truly understand what we were trying to say (or we might be sat there cringing, thinking that we didn't mean that). But also, it might be that we want someone else to talk to about decisions and choices, and to speak up for us. This is when an advocate could be useful, especially as they might have more ideas about what our rights are, and what options we have. Someone different can be extra helpful if the decision we're making is something that could affect you too, as then this can help us to think about what *we* really want, without having to worry about how you might feel about us talking of it with you.

> *If you have someone who can advocate on your behalf, that would be helpful, because then you don't feel as if you're doing it on your own.* (KIM)

Support for foster carers

We recognize that it's important that you, as our carers, also have enough support from the services around us, to know how you can best take care of us – so you feel equipped to talk to us about things and know how best to support us when we're struggling. You'll also need to know how to spot signs that we might need some extra support and be able to advocate for us to get this. If you don't know, then you can't help. You should feel able to ask for support or specify a training need – this stuff can feel difficult, or complex, so it's essential that you have the support that you need to know how to help us, because we're with you more than any other professional or service.

Summary

We often have so many services and professionals involved, but so much of what they do, and the meetings that we're asked to attend, can feel like a tick-box exercise. We can end up feeling like a number that no one's really listening to, rather than knowing that the conversations we have are meaningful. This can lead to us not wanting to get involved, or choosing carefully what to share with you and the professionals in these spaces. We would value you being alongside us with these services, thinking with us about what we want to get out of meetings, what we might want to say (or what we might want you to raise for us), and making sure that we think about what feels okay to bring into a meeting and what could be a conversation outside. One of the biggest things that you can support us with is helping us to make decisions, and listening when we have a view or ideas on things. This is also true when we are thinking about education, where we often make big decisions about our futures without much support. We discuss this further in the next chapter.

CHAPTER 8

Education and Finding a Way Out of the System

As the title of this chapter suggests, education is very important for children in care. It has the potential to be a safe space for us when things at home are a bit chaotic or challenging, and it can also be our 'way out' of the care system, helping us to feel more in control of what happens in our future lives. This chapter talks through some of the challenges that we might face when accessing education, and how you, as a foster carer, can help.

Why school is particularly important for us

> *School was my safe space because I had a really good pastoral team. There was so much going on, on the outside, with me moving about a lot, and school was my solid ground.*
> (AMY J)

Having an opportunity to get involved in education, and having support where needed to attend school, is important, but especially for young people in care. Often school may be our safe haven. Sometimes we find it difficult to be at home, and school may feel like an opportunity to get away for a while, a place where we can try to forget about the problems that we're facing at home. It can feel separate and safer, and somewhere where life might feel a bit more 'normal'. We might not want to talk in school about the difficulties at home, as this could bring our trauma or distress into the school environment too. As Kim suggests, 'If you mix the two, you can't escape it.' But at the same time, it's important for us to have space to talk when we're ready to, and it might be that our teacher or pastoral support is the person we feel safest to share our difficulties with. So it's important that we have space to talk if we wish to, but that this isn't forced on us.

School staff can also be another big part of our support network, because we spend so much time at school. If they genuinely care for us, they can often be there at the important times, and sometimes throughout our transitions. They can also support and guide us, and help us think through future decisions and challenges. Kim describes her sixth-form college teachers being alongside her ('in it with me') when she was considering what to do for university. They helped her to think through the pros, cons, limitations, and what kind of care leaver package of support each university had. They also supported her to attend an event about this, to help her to make good decisions.

> *I personally feel so grateful for my education. Still to this day, I absolutely love learning, and without this, I certainly wouldn't be where I am now. I would encourage every young person to invest in some form of education or learning.* (AMY)

School is also a way of supporting us to build our lives. As Kim said, 'If I wasn't educated, I wouldn't be where I am now.' Education brings opportunities and chances to take control and make changes in our lives. Even to work in fast-food outlets you now often need to get decent grades in your GCSEs. There's a danger that without any qualifications, we could end up turning to crime, especially if that's the way our families functioned. Education gives us a chance to do things differently. If you can support us to have a good education, and then a good job with good pay, this can be our way out of the care system, because we won't have to rely as much on social care going forward.

I was refusing to go out, so wouldn't have seen any other refugee, or teenager even, if I hadn't had school. School helped me learn the language. My foster dad pushed hard for me to do ESOL [English for Speakers of Other Languages] straight away, because I would have had to do A-levels when I was 17 [a year after arriving in the UK]. He pushed me to do my GCSEs in one year, because he knew I was bright and it was only the language giving me trouble. He pushed hard to do it and I achieved it. He pushed the system to recognize a young child, to allow me to have multiple routes and options through education, and to recognize my potential. (NOOR)

School can sometimes also help us to identify some of our strengths, give us a role that we value or an opportunity to step up into something. When Kim was able to get back into mainstream school, one of her teachers introduced her to a youth council, which allowed her to channel her energy and start to use her voice in a more positive way.

I guess that's where I really turned my whole life around, because it's the start of my advocacy work. It was the start of using my voice. It was the start of like, hey, this is a platform where I can help people. (KIM)

The educational challenges we face

We often have so many more stresses than other young people and they aren't always properly understood. For example, if we're going through exams, we may feel additional pressure to do well, but we might have missed lots of school or have been moving between schools, which can make our learning really fragmented and things much more difficult. We often may also be worrying about other things in our life too.

> *Stress starts to affect you from January, as you have January exams, you have June exams. But in my head, while I'm worrying about my exams, I'm worrying about where I am going to live. I have nowhere to go. Like these exams right now are not important if I don't have anywhere to live, if I'm going to be homeless. So yet again, it's just additional pressures that we have that other people don't have, and it affects our performance.* (KIM)

Other children can just focus on their schoolwork or study, whereas we may struggle to give this our full attention, due to multiple other factors within our life. It can feel as if we're always at a disadvantage within school, always playing 'catch up', which can be frustrating. Often, decisions can be made about our education, such as a move between schools, or a choice about which school we'll go to, without us being consulted. Not having a say in where we're going and what changes are made can feel unfair and as if we're even more powerless.

When we have to move school multiple times due to moving foster homes, this can be really stressful. Change is stressful to humans anyway because of the unknown and uncertainty. But on top of this, teaching styles and the syllabus also change between schools, so we're at a disadvantage and playing catch up, as well as having to navigate new social relationships and trying to fit in. This is in addition to coping with the changes and challenges that we're going through at home, which may include losses of relationships or a move to a new area. Education should be as flexible as possible around people's circumstances. Our priority might understandably not be education right now, when we're going through so many other major life experiences.

When you move schools a lot, your foster carer would have to take you to a new school, and you feel like you have just no one. You just need someone to sit down with you and ask if you are okay. (DIEGO)

Difficulties in school

We know there are lots of things that can affect our confidence in school. Multiple moves between homes, and often schools, can cause a lot of educational disruption. A lack of belief in ourselves generally, having a fear of failure or of not being good enough, can all impact our ability to focus or 'give it a go' in the classroom. Difficulties with emotions and concentration can make this even harder. All of these can impact our confidence in our abilities, and we may believe that we're not going to do well, which can end up being a self-fulfilling prophecy.

I've always felt that I'm not very intelligent and I have to work twice as hard as everybody else just to achieve the same as most people. This thought process has been with me for as long as I can remember, and I still find myself feeling this way now I'm an adult. (AMY)

When things are difficult at home, this can impact how we show up to school. Often if our 'behaviour' in school is poor, it can mean that we're struggling with things at home but are finding it tough to communicate how we're feeling.

> *In a way, when I think about it, it was a cry for help. Like, hey, I need help, I need support. But at that age, you don't really necessarily know how to ask for it.* (KIM)

Kim feels that she was 'channelling that energy in the wrong places and in the wrong way'. There's a danger that the school focuses on the behaviour, without thinking about where it's coming from and what might be going on for us.

> *I would get detentions on purpose so I didn't have to go back home to my foster carer, but then it would be even harder at home... I think they should sit down with the young person and ask them, 'What is on your mind? What can I help you with? Have you got any homework and can I help you with it?' Like you are going through the hardest time of your life in secondary school, you are starting periods, meeting new people. Especially when you have to move schools a lot, becoming more independent and you feel like you are doing it all alone, without your family. It's not easy. If they approached me calmly and talked to me about it rather than taking all my stuff off me and shouting at me, that would have been better. Just speak calmly and try and understand why I'm behaving how I'm behaving.* (DIEGO)

Sadly, when a child's behaviour in school doesn't meet the expectations of teachers, it can lead to them being excluded or expelled. When you're excluded, it can also lead to other people becoming frustrated with you, which can then make it feel even worse at school. As Kim shares below, this can have a detrimental impact on the child's opportunities going forward.

> *[the school was saying] Right now, we just can't manage you. And I think that was the worst decision they ever made for me, because then they put me into an environment where I was around kids who were getting in trouble all the time, and I knew that I was never like that. I felt like I'm just not like these people. Those kids didn't have a care in the world and that really impacted me, because it exposed me to that kind of behaviour, and I was like, well, if I'm in this environment, I'm just going to live up to that expectation because that's what you think of me anyway.* (KIM)

Why your support is so important

As we've discussed above, education can be a 'way out' for children in care, a way to move away from the known trajectory. However, if we feel as if this is another thing that we have to get through by ourselves, and we might not have the belief that we're able to do it well, then it might feel overwhelming, and we might want to give up. However, if we feel that you're alongside us through our educational journey, and understand why it might be challenging for us, this can feel supportive and make things feel a bit more manageable.

> *As soon as they [foster carer] have a child come to their care, they go to their school and ask all the obvious questions*

– how are they, are they struggling, do they like packed lunch/school dinners, how were they with previous carers, what was their routine, what did it look like, did they do after school clubs, is there anything else they want to do in school, how can the carers support them in school? Ask. The social worker might not know the child, but school will, and they will know a lot. So go in, go for a meeting, be assertive. Get a sense of the child's routine and try to match it. This is important, otherwise they're moving home and changing their whole routine, just because they are moving to a new place. For me, our new foster placement was about an hour away from school and because the carers worked in the day, we had to get taxis to and from school, which was a bit crazy. I had to get up an extra hour early, then do a whole day of school, then get a taxi back for an hour. Our routine wasn't the same as it was before, so that was draining and a lot. The taxi driver gave my brother a little red car he had on his dashboard when he stopped taking him to school. Obviously, he didn't know he was in care, and my brother kept it and talked about the red car through his life. Small things like that matter a lot. (SHANNON)

As Shannon says above, if we've been at the school for some time, asking them about us can be a good way of finding out more about us, our routines, our lives, and what's important to us. It can help you think about what we might get from school, any challenges we face, and how you can best support us to try to keep things the same as much as possible (if this is working), or tweak things to help us to feel more able to attend.

It also helps when you have a good understanding of why we might find attending school hard. Although it's helpful to be interested in where our skills lie, be hopeful and believe in us and our abilities, and encourage us to achieve, please be aware that if you put too much pressure on us, it'll feel like an extra stress that we really don't need.

> *It's important to focus on academic achievement, but it's not beneficial to put pressure on it, because pressure leads to cracks. And the last thing that anyone wants within that situation is for us to fall down and break apart. To help with that, it's support and encouragement. I remember not liking going to school, in primary and secondary. But in residential care, one of the first things that was asked of me was what was my favourite subject. Then when I returned from school, they always asked me about how I'd found that subject, what I had learned. They recognized what I enjoyed, and then tried to feed into and nurture that area – I really appreciated that.* (CJ)

When high expectations are set for us which we seem unlikely to achieve, this is unhelpful. It feels very demeaning when we know that there's a target and we can't reach it, which can make us feel bad about ourselves. It can make us feel that we're not doing well at all, or that we're not good enough. Then it's likely that we might lose motivation and give up trying, and are left feeling not great. However, when we're asked what we want to do and are supported to set our own targets, we're given a sense of agency, which can lead to internal drive and direction.

When you can attend school/college open days, and parents' evenings, with us, that can feel massively supportive. Everyone else will be taking their mum or dad, which feels much more normal, so it can be terrifying for us to go on our own. If it's visiting a new place, this is especially important as it can feel like a whole new world, so it's nice to have someone with us to take away a bit of the worry and help us to feel more confident. This is really important.

When we're a bit older, sometimes you might think that you need to step back and allow us just to get on with our education, thinking that we can do it ourselves (especially if we seem like quite an independent person). However, often we might still need some support and might really appreciate encouragement and recognition of when we might be struggling and with what, and when we're doing well. For example, coming to parents'/carers' evenings and exam results days is still important. Where you can take an interest in our education, it can make such a difference to us.

Supporting us to make choices in education

Often, educational decisions (like choosing subjects or thinking about which courses we want to go on) can feel a bit much or overwhelming for us. We might be living mainly in the here-and-now, as life has been so changeable, and we might not know where we'll be living in a year's time, and whether we'll still have your support or we'll be alone again. Even if you say to us that you're not going to give up on us, we might struggle to believe this based on what has happened to us before, so things might still feel unstable. This lack of stability can therefore lead to additional pressures for us. These educational decisions can be such big life choices, and there's a danger that we may feel that we're having to make these decisions alone. It might be that we don't even know where to start making these decisions.

> *I just picked what I was interested in, rather than thinking about where it would lead to.* (AMY)

One thing to consider is that even if we sound confident in our educational choices, we might not be. We could have learned over time to be self-sufficient as we've been unable to rely on adults in our life to be around and support us. Therefore, we might have learned that we need to do things alone and make our own decisions. This apparent confidence could mean that you step back and allow us to get on with it. However, it might be that despite this, we'd really value your support. Making these decisions can feel *such* a big thing to do alone. Being curious and exploring our options with us can be helpful. It might also help to be a little vulnerable yourself, talking about how you've found making decisions like this difficult too, for example, to show that you get that this is a big decision and can be a bit scary.

Choosing what to do next: Further education

If possible, the option of having a coach, tutor or mentor, who can talk to us about different educational/vocational options and the different routes that we could take, would be useful.

> *In terms of studying and picking my A-levels, I just picked what I was good at and what I enjoyed. I didn't necessarily think of the job that it would lead to.* (KIM)

It might be difficult for us to think about our future, especially if a lot of the things in our life have been so changeable and unstable, so we may benefit from some support to think things through, such as the consequences of different decisions and routes. Having these conversations with us from a secondary school age can help us to be more informed and enable us to make good decisions for our future. We may sometimes push against this but knowing you're there and want to help can be useful. It can also be helpful to get access to careers advice from people who've worked with care-experienced people before, so that they can let us know about what opportunities might be out there, including scholarships and apprenticeships, and other things that we might not have thought about before.

If we're not considering further education or study, it can also help to explore the reasons why. We may be fearful of another move or worry that we'll not be able to handle the pressure, or may be unsure of the financial implications. There might be a worry about potential debt, which may lead us to think, 'Oh my gosh, I can't afford it!' It can therefore be useful to know what support we would be entitled to if we were to progress, as lots of people won't be aware of what's out there. Also, by having these conversations, you're showing that you believe in us and that we can do it if we want to.

Top tip

Care-experienced young people can often be eligible for financial support such as bursaries, scholarships, and sponsorships when accessing further education. There can be apprenticeships available specifically for care-experienced young people. There also may be additional opportunities for support within a university setting. Therefore, if the child you're supporting is thinking about accessing further education, it can be useful to liaise with care-experienced organizations, and the universities, to find out more.

With decisions like going to university, there can be a lot of compromise and challenges. It can impact our ability to get more permanent housing; it can mean another significant move, and leaving people with whom we've started to build relationships. It can mean having to grow up quickly and live more independently, but we may not have the adult support around us that our peers have. We would need to decide whether we want to stay off campus or move into halls to get the 'full uni' experience. Kim decided to move into halls, 'For once, wanting to feel normal like the rest of my peers.' We also need to consider what we'll do during the university holidays.

> *The worst ones have to be Easter and the summer holidays. The Easter period is typically a month off for you where yet again everyone goes back home. But the good thing is you still have your accommodation so you can stay at uni, but you'll just stay there by yourself, which is so lonely... In the summer, a lot of university contracts are from, say, September, October up until June. So that means that from the end of June through to September you're kind of homeless and those four months you just have to navigate things yourself. I was sofa surfing wherever anyone could take me or wherever it was low cost.* (KIM)

Also, going to university can be expensive, with the cost of accommodation in halls too. Kim ended up sofa surfing at times, staying with friends who had spare rooms, beds, or sofas. This was very stressful, the constant living out of suitcases, not knowing where she was going. Kim recalls going to London one day with two suitcases and no idea where she was going, crying in the station, and thinking, 'I'm in London and I don't know where I will sleep tonight.' She speaks about how during the holidays, everyone else goes home, 'It's just you, and mentally that's so hard to be the only one there.' So if you are able to, as foster carers, offer some ongoing help or advice while we are at university, this can be so valuable, and such a support to help us get through it.

> *I technically did leave (foster care) at 18 but I wasn't fully gone. I still left all my things in my room. I left most of my clothes and my bedroom the same while I was at uni, so I'd just go back there when I needed to go back to be with my (foster) family and I wanted to go home. I can't imagine not having a space to go back to. I was lucky that I had the option to go back to my foster carers. I always had a place to stay. As a care leaver, moving out without somewhere to fall back on, you can end up feeling lonely and lost. If I was stressed at university I could go back for the weekend. I relied on my foster carers a lot too, for advice, or if I ran out of money they would give me, like, £20. The relationships students have with their parents, I had that with my foster carers. You're still really young when you go to uni, and you still need that support from your carers and guardians.*
> **(ANGEL)**

Summary

Education is a big part of young people's lives growing up, but for young people in care, it can be a safe haven when things at home are tough. It can create more opportunities and become a way of getting out of the social care system, allowing us to make decisions about where we want our life to go in the future. However, it can also be more difficult for us within school, as we often have so many other stressful things happening at the same time, so it can be hard to prioritize our education. Typically, young people have lots of support around education and decision making, so it's important that we have support from those around us too, helping us to know what our options are, and what might be available to us, so that we can make informed choices. As we get older and potentially leave your care, we might also have big decisions to make about further education, if this is something that we want. But there are other things that we need to consider about this, such as where we live, finances, and the relationships that we've made. In the next chapter, we continue to think about the many challenges that we might have when we're leaving care, and how you can support us with them.

CHAPTER 9

Leaving Home with Dignity

When people talk about 'leaving home', they're normally referring to leaving home as an adult, which is a time that's usually exciting. It's a time to have your own space, your independence, and choice about what your future looks like. It's a bit different when you're in care. Some of us may be lucky and have supportive foster families to help us with the next steps, but others of us won't have that support. Some of us will end up moving on from homes where our carers may have been talking and preparing for us to move out for quite some time, even discussing what they'll be doing with our room when we leave. This can help in some ways, as we can build up life skills and independence, and process the loss of the relationship ahead of time, but it can also leave us feeling rejected or abandoned. Others of us will have brilliant foster carers, who keep our room set up as 'our room' to come back to long after we leave – just like in a 'real' family. But we realize that this isn't always possible. In this chapter, we'll explore what it's like to leave home, acknowledge some of the key challenges including those that might be unavoidable, and think about how you can support us through this time, with dignity, care, and respect.

> *My experience of leaving my foster home was a difficult one as I had voluntarily signed to be in care, which meant I was able to sign myself out, which I did at 16. Following this, I ended up homeless and, eventually, after lots of sleeping on people's floors, I ended up living in a supported accommodation. When I look back on this, I think if I'd have had more support around what I felt I needed, this would have likely changed the outcome.* (MIA)

You don't get a choice

It's hard to feel as if you don't have any choice in what's happening next when you're living in care, away from your family. We might not want to move, we might not feel ready to, or the options shared with us might be so bad we can't imagine anything worse. When we have to move out, aged 16, 17, or 18, into supported accommodation, a hostel, or our own tenancy, some of the places we're shown (usually by our social worker or personal advisor) are not nice, especially if we've been used to living in a nice home and/or nice area. It's seems as if everyone has forgotten that we were put in care to protect us from harmful environments, but then when we turn 18, they put us back in those very same, or other unsafe, environments. It's not where we want to be as a young person. And we can be vulnerable, because we often don't have a family to support us, so we might be looking for a family (or love or care) in the people we meet – our 'chosen family'. But when the only options we see are in run-down areas, with people involved in crime, then we might end up involved in crime too. Where we live is so important. We want to be surrounded by good, supportive people, and we want to feel safe at home. We don't want to go back to an environment that's similar to where we were taken from and repeat the cycle.

> *You're on the list for months for the housing association, and then if you say no, they put you to the bottom of the list and treat you like you're being difficult. But I wasn't. I was scared because those places they showed me didn't feel safe, they felt intimidating.* (ANGEL)

If that happens, it might well have been expected, because some of us won't hold hopes and aspirations for a better life. When we've had a difficult childhood and not had the best opportunities, or been shown our potential, then we're not going to have high expectations of where we could be living. Or some of us may have been taught that we deserve more, and we may have started to believe that, but then that can make it even harder to be shown poor housing options. It's not that we're entitled, but...would you want your child living there?

It was terrifying, to be honest with you. My head started to figure out what was going on. Like you're an adult. How come in one night you can be an adult? It's a lot to take in. It was not nice. I had to figure out myself what I was responsible for. I had to book all my own appointments by myself and arrange them. Important Home Office appointments. My foster family were great and I went back to them for a few days to stay. They spoke to my new home before I moved in to check it was okay for me and they knew what I needed. I think they should have started the process from when I turned 17. I would have still had foster family support then, so when I moved out it wouldn't have been as shocking. My foster family, I still regularly go to them and they visit me. Most of the time I spend with them actually. Somehow they adopted me. (NOOR)

When trying to find a home, there's also a stigma about being in care that's difficult to get away from, no matter what you do or say. Being care experienced isn't a protected characteristic throughout the UK (although a number of councils have now recognized it as a protected characteristic within their locality – which we would fully support and think is a good step forward). This means that you can be discriminated against for being care experienced, and you're powerless to do anything about it.

For example, if you're a homeless 18-year-old and have to go to a private rental landlord who asks for your residential history, they might realize that you're a care leaver and decide not to house you.

When you're in care, this often isn't the first time we've had to 'leave home'. Our first time will likely have involved us leaving our parents. And then we might have had a few moves, between different foster carers, spending time with short breaks (or respite) carers, or even moving into and out of children's homes.

> *I always remember it being so traumatic. It wasn't nice to move from one home into another. And for us, we always spent at least a year with families before moving; you are just getting comfortable and then you're moving again. I always left crying my eyes out and feeling petrified – really scared and anxious, like I had no idea where I was going or what was happening.* (ANGEL)

Below we share some of our thoughts on what can help when we need to move home. While this is usually inevitable, it doesn't have to be traumatic. Following this advice can help us leave home in the best way, with dignity.

Starting the process early

When we say early, we mean even before we move in. As we shared in Chapter 2 (Going into a Stranger's Home), when you're moving into a new home, with a brand-new family, it's scary and you've no idea what to expect. We don't know who you are, whether we'll like you or your family, whether you'll like us, what it's going to be like living with you – and the big question, how long it will be before we're asked to leave. It can help to talk about endings and leaving, right from the moment we move in with you. We'll be thinking about it anyway, so it's helpful if we can name it and talk about it together.

> *Foster carers need to have clarity and honesty with the young person from the outset because if they don't know what's going on in advance, having to move feels sudden. Even if they're not sure how long the young person will be living with them, they could say something like, 'You can only stay here for a set amount of time. We can't tell you how much, and we will have you as long as we can but it will have an end point.' You need to have that clarity; it helps the child understand. It's just honesty. They have to put themselves in that child's position to feel those emotions that the young person is feeling.* (SHANNON)

Be open, honest, and clear

Imagine if you were told you had to leave home and move to somewhere new, potentially far away, meaning you'd have to leave your friends, family, and job behind, but you weren't told where. Now imagine that you weren't told when, and you were picked up from work by someone you didn't know that well and told you would be moving somewhere new. What would it feel like? What would be running through your head? What would you do?

We understand it can be hard to share bad news with someone you care about. Maybe it's not a decision you felt part of or agreed with and wanted. But it's important that this doesn't get in the way of us being involved in, or told about, the most important pieces of information in our life. And knowing where we're going to be living (or not living) is pretty important. Be clear, calm, and compassionate, and understand that we might get upset – wouldn't you get upset too? Would you want that to stop someone telling you?

If people are saying they don't want to tell them because they'd get upset, that can be the carer protecting themselves from the child being upset. Being told in advance helps you to come to terms with it. It's important that carers think about how they will manage explaining to the child about change, which might lead to them not being their foster carers. They can't allow their own emotions to be involved. The child will be ten times more upset thinking that you don't want them or that you've hidden something from them and not involved them if you suddenly say, 'Oh sorry, you've got to go now.' (SHANNON)

See our potential

As we described earlier in the book, living in care, we might not have the highest expectations of ourselves, and might not think we are worth much, and other people might not believe in us either. We might expect the worst from ourselves, from others around us, and from life in general. So we need you, as our carers, to be able to hold hope for us, show that you believe in us, and see potential options that we can take that we might not see for ourselves. As we discussed in the last chapter, going to university might not be something we expect to achieve ourselves, so it can help us to know that it's an option. It might not be an option we'd like to pursue and that's okay too, but it's good to know someone is seeing our potential, even when we don't see it ourselves. It's the same when we think about housing options. We might not fully understand what we're entitled to, so we need help from you as our carers, to make sure we understand our rights, and to advocate for us, and help us to know that we have a choice. It might be that you can see a way of helping us with our housing options when we move out at 18, when we might think we have to go wherever we are given.

> *I wasn't given an option that helped me to feel I was in a safe and secure place to be. I found that by myself, with my foster carers. They helped me to move in with my foster sibling Gia. It really helped knowing I wasn't moving out to live completely by myself. I think it helps to move out with friends and foster siblings, as having that support makes it easier. You could get lonely moving out by yourself. You have to live by yourself when you move with the housing association, and my support worker was really focused on me living alone. I had to fight for my full bursary because I wasn't living on my own. You're doing so much for the first time, so having someone to live with can really help. I'm glad I had the assertiveness to say no, that's not what I wanted. My foster carer made me realize that wasn't my only option. It helped that I had someone to say that I didn't have to do that; I had the autonomy to choose.* (ANGEL)

Take time and plan

It doesn't matter which move we're talking about. Whether moving out of our carer's home and the care system completely, moving between foster homes or children's homes, or even going to stay with some short-break carers, it's important to take a bit of time where possible to plan this big change.

One week, my social worker just went, 'Right, you need to pack up your stuff and we will take you.' They didn't give me the chance to think about it or prepare; they could have been taking me anywhere. The second to last home I was in, my social worker came to me and told me, 'We need to move you and there's no homes, so we've got to move you to a completely different city.' And I refused. And I stood there and made him find me a place in my area. If the foster carer knows that the child could be moving to a different carer or going into residential then they could go and visit it with them, to explain about it – what it's like, where it is, what will happen. Say, 'This is where you are gonna be' because if the child feels safe with that carer, then it's going to help them that their carer has been to this new place. It might help them feel safe there too. (SHANNON)

If the move is planned, and you know about it in advance, it's important to have ongoing conversations with us about it. If we have a good relationship, it's going to help if you can check in with us about how we're feeling about the move, and any worries we might have (we might not tell you, unless you ask, and might keep it in).

It might be that the move is under quite difficult or awkward circumstances. Maybe it's been decided that we have to move on because there are worries about our safety, or your safety, or maybe we've signed ourselves out of your care. When this happens, it's just about doing what you can, being empathic and kind, and trying not to show any animosity. It's probably going to be difficult for both of us. Or it might be that it's time for us to leave, and we're both feeling sad, upset, or worried about this ending.

It's helpful if we know that you're by our side through this no matter what, and that you still care. Maybe ask us if there's any information we want to find out and help us to ask our social worker if we need your support to do this. Ask us if there's anything that we're going to need to take with us, or give suggestions of things that we might not have thought about yet.

Although you might jump into wanting to tell us about the plans, it's usually best if these come from our social worker or personal advisor. They need to be the people telling us the plans for the move, any decisions that have been made, and why. But you might be able to help us to think about what we want to ask, anything we're not sure about, and to be someone that we can talk to about how we're feeling about it. We could end up feeling angry towards the person who gives us this information, so it's best if it's not you. We'll need you for support.

Then you can also help us to prepare and to pack. Get us suitcases or bags and help us (if we want you to) to pack in good time, and make sure that we know where all our important things are. Then you could offer to help us unpack in our new home, making sure we've got everything we need, and supporting us to buy anything we don't have. If you can, help us to make it feel as much like home as possible and personalize it with things that are ours, or new things that we've chosen.

If we're moving to somewhere we don't want to go, or somewhere that feels like a 'bad' move, then it's likely that we're going to feel awful about it. Try to stay balanced where you can, so that you can acknowledge the challenges with us, but also see some potential positives too. One of the biggest things is if you can support us to stay in touch with our important people, including you, where we can and want to.

Support us to build our skills

We might be 18 and technically 'an adult' when we're moving into our own home, and we might feel old enough, but 18 is actually still quite young. So while we might be excited about the good parts of moving out, buying furniture and paint, there's a lot we might still not know we need to think about. We need someone there to support us through the move, to help us to troubleshoot any challenges as they come up, someone we can call to ask questions about bills – gas, electricity, water. Some of us have had our foster carers to support us in learning life skills, but others may have been sheltered from it, meaning it comes as a complete shock when we move out.

> *You feel like you're out there, in the middle of the world by yourself, and you feel really sad and anxious and alone, if you don't have a home and a family to fall back on.* **(ANGEL)**

It's really helpful when you can step in and support us with things sometimes, especially when we are feeling alone and everything around us seems quite overwhelming. But, as tempting as it is, please try to hold off from 'fixing it' for us all the time. We don't learn anything when you do everything for us. Some of the best examples of how carers have helped us have involved them allowing us to struggle with it a little, teaching us, and guiding us with what we need to do, but letting us even fail a bit (with the carer as our safety net), so that we can learn and do better next time.

> *Whatever it is, my foster family always tell me I can do it. They do see this for me even when I struggle to see what I am capable of. I wish I could see myself through their eyes – it's like magic lenses. They say, 'Even if you don't know the language or the system, you can do this.' And they let*

me struggle with it until I figure it out on my own. My foster dad says when you learn by yourself, or in the hard way, you will appreciate more and will make sure next time you do well, and I don't agree with him, but I know it does make me more independent. (NOOR)

Choice and control

It helps when it's our decision to move out, and we can decide on things like where and with whom we will live next. When we don't have that choice, it's still important to involve us, ask us how we feel about the move, and give us options. Often we might feel that this is being 'done to' us, and we're being told what's going to happen without us having any choice or say. Because of this, we can end up in a situation that won't work, and everyone might end up feeling as if they've 'failed'.

It helped that it was my decision when to move out. I was lucky that I had the opportunity to do it that way, as care leavers often have to do it on their 18th birthday. It helps you when you have control and autonomy over your own life. That's what made the move positive, not negative. I was excited to move out, excited to get furniture and move into my own place. It helped to have support as I was moving. I could call my carers to ask about things like gas, electricity, and water bills. If you don't have your foster carers, you need it from someone, so you'd need to know who. (ANGEL)

When moving home, it doesn't help when our sense of agency is taken away from us; for example, when other people go through and pack up our things for us. This gets in the way of our sense of closure. Some of the most difficult moves occur when we've not been aware that they're going to happen. Sometimes it might be that we go to school and then find out that we're being taken somewhere else, and we don't even get the chance to say goodbye, see our room, pack up our possessions. This gives us no time to mentally prepare to go into a new environment or say goodbye to our last home.

Stay in touch/be there to fall back on

> *One thing that was a great relief to me was them saying that they will always be there...they are only up the road from me now. I'd still pass them if I was going to do my groceries, and I could give them a wave, or knock on their door and have a five-minute conversation. Knowing there will always be someone there who knows you, and will miss you, and miss your company, that's a great comfort.* (CJ)

When we don't have family to fall back on, and we've spent years building trust in our foster carers, it can feel soul destroying when we turn 16 or 18 and that support falls away. This might mean that we then don't have any support, but even if we do, it can still feel as if we've been let down and abandoned by the people who told us we could trust them, or that they don't care enough to stay in contact with us. Where there is a possibility of keeping this relationship going in some way, it can make a real difference – whether this is just keeping in touch or visiting each other, or us being able to reach out for support from you. Having someone to fall back on is so important.

Keeping in touch is so crucial... I think caring, compassionate, considerate carers will want to stay in touch – like let them visit or visit them and catch up. This is especially important if the young person has lived there for a long time. I wish I could somehow find my first carers and thank them for that short period of time because I will never forget it. Every little thing that we used to do with them, even down to being in the garden, picking raspberries, making crumble. It's these little, seemingly insignificant things that matter and stay in your memory, especially if it was a good experience. Children do remember it. (SHANNON)

When done well, this can lead to meaningful and longstanding relationships for us. Noor is still in contact with her foster carers.

I am still in contact with them, by the way, and they are still my family now. Legally I was out, but any time between my A-levels and university or whatever, I go back to their house. (NOOR)

I still see my foster carers sometimes, which is lovely, and it should still be on offer as standard. There have been times when I have not been ready to have that relationship, but I am now. That sense of belonging through relationships... The last time I went to see them, my foster carer got out a letter that I sent to him years and years ago and I was shocked to find I meant that much. (AMY)

How to say goodbye

When having to move, it can really help if we have something to take with us from our time in the foster home, something that helps us to say goodbye. Some of us have had scrapbooks made for us, with letters and notes and pictures in them, which can mean a lot. Photo albums or memory boxes can be great too. These are things we'll keep and look back through, to remember and reflect on some of the genuine relationships and memories from our time with you. It helps us to know that we'll be missed, and for you to know you'll be missed by us too. As memories, even good memories, can be fleeting, it's so valuable to have something physical to look through.

Summary

Just as coming into a new home is scary and overwhelming, leaving one is too. Often, we don't even get time to feel sad, because we're just so focused on processing the fear and anxiety about where we'll be living next. Moving is one of the hardest and most traumatic parts of being in care and it's important that these transitions are taken seriously, with consideration, compassion, and above all, time. We hope we've shared some helpful thoughts on what can help when planning an ending and a move. In the next chapter, we'll leave you with some parting words of wisdom from many of us who have contributed to this book.

CHAPTER 10

Parting Words of Wisdom

Now you've arrived at the end of the book, we hope that reading through the experiences, quotes, and advice has helped you to reflect on your journey as a foster carer, and given you some ideas for how you can best care for the children you look after. As we've mentioned throughout, you can make such a positive difference in the lives of your foster children if you try your best to understand us as individuals, stay patient, show us genuine care, and be alongside us throughout our time with you and beyond. Our time in foster care can be really difficult. It's so weird and stressful moving into a stranger's home, especially when we don't know all the unsaid rules and boundaries, and things can feel so new and alien. We'll also be carrying with us our histories and stories, the good, the bad, and the mundane. It's important that you let us lead in what we want to share with you, and when, but that you're also wanting to talk about and remember the good stuff too, and find out more about what makes us, us. In the book, we've talked about how essential our relationships and networks are, and we need you to help us to keep these, and reconnect with our people, and build authentic relationships that will be there when we eventually leave care. You can help us to see and feel what good, healthy relationships are like, and support us around developing these going forward, showing us that we're worthy of them. We feel more comfortable and confident in professional meetings when we know that you have our back, and are there to support us. When we can be helped to raise our views, we can assert our choices where we can, rather than feeling that things are being 'done to' us, or that we're just a number or a tick-box exercise. In education, too, we appreciate you being beside us, showing interest, giving us encouragement and guidance, while holding a bigger picture, as this can be such a good opportunity for us to get some power and control back. Then at the end of the day, when we're finally leaving your home, this can be difficult, awkward, emotional, or all three. But the best thing that you can do at this time is to help us to leave home with dignity, worth, and your unconditional support.

Thanks for reading this book.

We want to leave you with these parting words of wisdom from young people who've been in care (what they would most want you to keep in mind), to help you on your foster caring journey...

> If it's not good enough for your own child, it's not good enough for a foster child. (SHANNON)

> Don't ask too many questions when getting to know the young person. It can be overwhelming for the young person and sometimes feel like an invasion of privacy. Instead, prompt the young person to lead conversations as this would be the best way to get to know their likes and dislikes. Engage with the young person as much as possible and don't let them sit alone in their bedroom as this can be an isolating place for them. They may struggle to engage at first but just know that they are grateful for the effort you put into getting to know them even if they don't show it. (AMY J)

> Carers should reassure the young person by saying things like, 'I'm always going to be here for you', 'You're not alone and I understand that this is going to be hard for you', 'If you need to talk to someone, I'm here for you.' The young person would want to know if the foster carer is going to provide them with stability. (DIEGO)

> Show compassion and caring and help me towards getting help. (TERRY BIRKETT)

> That I'd grow up and be seen and have just that little more continued support to help achieve would have made the world of

difference if only you hadn't given me away. That you can make a lifetime of difference for a child by committing to continued care and love and support. Please be strong and even in the difficult times of caring for us, continue to fight, don't give up on us. It's worth getting all the support to continue to care for us. Ask for that support; talk with the child and social workers, and the team around you. I feel the damage more from my foster carers giving me away than I do from my birth family who had no team around or support network or financial ability. Help us no matter how hard it can be at times. We really are worth it. (ZENA)

I wish my carers knew that I was (and still am) different. But I have always wanted the things that make me who I am and make me different to be supported and treated in a positive light. Please don't make me hide who I am and mould me to be someone I am not. (ZAHRA)

As a society and especially as members of the caring profession, we need to acknowledge that the care experience doesn't end at 18; it lasts a lifetime. While in care, the opportunity is to create memories and enduring relationship, built on care and love. The privilege of the carer role is the influence of the developmental progress. Children in care must have the psychological safety to practise new skills that support them as they grow. The greatest amount of energy should be invested in the transitional time. We should always hold in mind children in care, transition from care: the point where dependence and attachments shift to independence and adulthood. This has been a time described as rushed and this is not what we would expect for our own children, so we must strive for prolonged experience of transition, which includes skill acquisition. We then know we are equipping young people as they enter early adulthood. Independence will only ever be achieved by establishing interdependence: the building and rebuilding of relationships. Good quality, reliable relationships last a lifetime too. (**MIKE S, CARE-EXPERIENCED SOCIAL WORKER**)

Be more emotionally available; don't just treat them like a kid you have to care for. Kids like us have had fucked up lives in respect of trauma and life shit. You won't know what they went through, or what they are still going through, and they might not want to talk about it, or even talk to you at all! They might have been thrown out or fled home or felt abandoned by their family and environment, and then they go into a foster family, and they might be like, 'Oh, are they gonna be like that?' Just be there, show that you're there and that you care, even if they say they don't want it. Just be more emotionally available and use your body language to show you are giving love and that you're not strangers. It's important to be human. And remember, not everyone is the same. Because some kids are not lucky enough. Life from both sides could have fucked them up. First, they had terrible parents or an environment that led to the care system. Or from a young age they have been there, and they don't know nothing except foster families and the care system, but they've been abused by their foster family and the system, or moved around a lot so they are just exhausted. Or kids like me who have come to the UK and need to learn both culture and language. Don't get me wrong, it's luxury that the care system is available, and I am one of the lucky ones and blessed to have had a good experience... But there are lots of stories from kids like me where their story was quite sad. (**NOOR**)

Try your best to make the child you are fostering feel welcomed and wanted. A lot of the time, especially if you're being passed around from placement to placement, you feel as though you don't fit in anywhere. When I moved in with my foster carers, they always told me they would care for us like we were their own, and that was something I had never heard before from foster carers. Usually you get labelled as the 'foster child' and that used to make me feel less than, in some ways, and even embarrassed. So I think that making your foster child feel at home and comfortable is the most important thing and really helps build relationships. (ANGEL)

At the end of the day, you are not trying to replace being a parent, a guardian, or a carer. The ultimate goal should be to show this person that you have taken into your life what a healthy dynamic and family looks like, even if it is not by blood. It's all about stopping the root cause of the problem – in reality that is the start of the problem, people being within those unhealthy environments. And if they are not healed or resolved, then that behaviour, whether it is learned or internalized, will carry on. But if you are taught that there is a different way of doing things, that you can live life in peace, then that's way better. (CJ)

Every child or young person you come across during your time of being a foster carer will have had their own individual experiences which have shaped them, and you should always try to respond to them with kindness and compassion. It's important to acknowledge that your journey as a foster carer will likely not always be straightforward, but you will be having a huge impact on a child or young person's life, so please make sure your reasons for being a foster carer are the right ones. And lastly, if you decide to foster children or young people, please be patient and don't give up on them, because they may need you more than they're willing to say. (AMY)

The decision to foster a young person is a profound and life-changing choice. By opening your home and heart, you offer them safety, love, and the chance for a brighter future. While fostering can come with its own set of challenges, the positive impact you make outweighs them. Many of these young individuals have faced difficult beginnings, but through fostering, you have the power to rewrite their stories, providing them with the stability, care, love, and security they deserve. The difference you can make in their lives is not just significant – it's transformative. Join us in helping to 'fix' this broken system by showing love and care to young people in foster care. (KIM)

Appendix I

Further reading and resources

John-Baptiste, A. (2024). *Looked After: A Childhood in Care*. Hodder & Stoughton.

Pierre, R. (ed.) (2024). *Free Loaves on Fridays: The Care System as Told by People Who Actually Get It*. Unbound.

Sissay, L. (2020). *My Name Is Why*. Canongate Books.

Whitbread, F. (2024). *My Bright Shining Star*. Words & Pictures.

Websites for support and guidance

https://corambaaf.org.uk

www.childrenscommissioner.gov.uk/help-at-hand

https://becomecharity.org.uk

www.nyas.net/get-support/young-people/your-rights-and-entitlements

Acknowledgements

We would like to say a big thanks to all the young people and adults who contributed their thoughts, views, reflections, and stories to this book, including Angel, Noor, Amy J, Diego, Dave, Mike S, Rebecca, Rosie, Shannon, Jo, Zoe, Zena, Zahra, Terry, and Mia.

Kim

First, I would like to thank God for His consistency and provision, guiding me through the darkest years of my life and helping me overcome every obstacle I have faced. His presence and grace have brought me to where I am today, and I am forever grateful for His love. Second, I want to express my gratitude to my guardian angel, my mother. I know that I am standing in her prayers, which have sustained me since 1997. My mother has always been my driving force, motivating me to strive for the best in myself and inspiring me to work towards fixing a broken system. Thank you, Mum, for teaching me the importance of using my voice and advocating for change. I am also incredibly thankful for the people, organizations, and communities that God has provided me with over the years, helping me navigate life. I am grateful to every single person who has poured into me and stood by me. While I wish I could mention everyone by name, it would be impossible to list you all. However, I want to take this opportunity to publicly acknowledge Antonia Barnes-Christian and Deborah Colombeau for their unconditional love and support over the years.

Amy

I first want to thank my beautiful children, Autumn and Alister. You will forever be the reason I aim to be the best version of me, and I owe all of my successes to you both. Autumn, with your kind heart and thoughtfulness, and Alister, with your free-spirited nature and strength, you continue to inspire me every day. I also want to thank my incredible partner and better half, Samuel. Your confidence and positivity are unmatched, and you have always supported me to never give up on my dreams. I will forever be grateful for all you do. Also, to my bonus child, Izabella, your confidence and humour add so much joy to my life, thank you. Lastly, although there are too many to name, I would like to thank each and every individual who has believed in me, supported me, and inspired me along my journey so far.

CJ

I would like to thank Culland House and Homes for Support for taking care of me when I was going through an incredibly rough period of my life. I would like to thank my friends and found family for showing me that it isn't blood that makes your commitment. And I would like to thank everybody else involved in the process for this creation, and the reader.

Laura

I thank Kim, Amy, and CJ for their commitment and wisdom in crafting this book. The biggest thanks to them, and all of the young people involved, for so many interesting, enlightening, and inspiring conversations. I do hope we have done them justice.

Sue

I would like to thank all the people who have dedicated both time and headspace to contribute to this book, and those who have shared a little of themselves and their experiences. Kim, Amy, CJ, and all other contributors, I have learned so much from listening to you, and I feel really honoured to be part of this project. Thanks for taking a leap of faith with us.

A big thanks to our draft readers Jess, Katy, Carole, and Jane, for your support and encouragement, valuable feedback, and enthusiasm about the project. A massive thanks to Richard, for beautifully illustrating each chapter. And finally, to Amy and Steve at Jessica Kingsley Publishers, for believing in us and this book, and Sarah for your thorough, thoughtful editorial support.